JESUS IS NO JOKE

PRAISE FOR JESUS IS NO JOKE

A raw outpouring of pure emotion from someone who is hardly a member of the clergy - "*Jesus is No Joke: A True Story of an Unlikely Witness Who Saw Jesus*" is the tale of Heidi Hollis and her religious experience after one random nap – which revolutionized her life and changed it forever. She explains what she saw and pours out real, true emotion – with little political motivation that one so often hears from the ordained clergy. An inspiring and encouraging tale for spiritual people, "*Jesus is No Joke: A True Story of an Unlikely Witness Who Saw Jesus*" is a must for community library spirituality and Christian studies collections.

~James A. Cox, Editor-in-Chief ~*Midwest Book Review*

I am the editor and co-founder of a spiritual magazine, *Pure Inspiration*, so what I do day in and day out is read books, articles, and other materials pertaining to spiritual matters. Much of what I receive is, frankly, not of great interest to me. Having said that, I recently received Heidi Hollis' book, Jesus Is No Joke, and began to read it. It was so good that I took it home and read the entire book within a day or two. Heidi's writing style simply drew me in -- it's natural, refreshingly "real," and enthusiastic. Best of all, she has something to say. Her encounters with Jesus were riveting and inspiring and they conveyed, above all, the feeling of Jesus' reality. Heidi writes from her heart, her soul, and after reading this book, I felt that I knew her, appreciated her, and admired her courage. A must-read for those who seek the Light.

~Robert Becker/Editor, *Pure Inspiration Magazine*

Does God still directly reveal Himself out of the blue to people 2000+ years after the Bible was completed? You bet! Heidi was given the rare privilege of meeting the resurrected Lord in these final days before His return to earth. Her book is a colorful spiritual journal, well written in a unique casual style - making it an easy read. I am one who reads books on the supernatural to get new revelations from God, and I found a lot of these golden nuggets of God-given tips on living a meaningful victorious life in this book. This is a must read for all who live their lives without taking the Author of Life seriously. Thanks Heidi for sharing your personal encounter with the Man Himself.

~ Zaldy Andales, EndTimeRevelations.org

Heidi Hollis does a fantastic job bringing a difficult and emotional subject down to the level of explanation and understanding it has been lacking. The book has a great flow to it with stories of her experiences that obviously had a profound effect on her. One of the best things about "JINJ" is the feeling you get that Heidi is sitting right in front you sharing this, wanting you to be a part of the journey and relive it with her through the pages. It truly has that kind of personal feel to it. While reading "JINJ" you will find yourself not believing and then believing, laughing and smiling and feeling uplifted by the words that cover the pages. In my opinion this is a front row seat into the mind of Heidi Hollis and her inspirations. You can honestly envision her typing the words as you read.

~Jeremiah Greer, Editor-in-Chief ~*Mysteries Magazine*/Host of *Shadows In The Dark Radio*

JESUS IS NO JOKE

A True Story
OF AN UNLIKELY WITNESS
WHO SAW JESUS

HEIDI HOLLIS

Level Head
Publishing
www.levelheadpublishing.com

Jesus Is No Joke:
A True Story of an Unlikely Witness Who Saw Jesus
Copyright 2008, 2011 by Heidi Hollis
First published March 21st, 2008

Scripture is taken from the Holy Bible, King James Version (KJV)

JINJ E-Book - ISBN: 978-0-9830401-0-1

JINJ Softcover - ISBN: 978-0-615-19005-1

JINJ Hard Cover - ISBN: 978-0-9830401-2-5

Level Head Publishing books may be ordered through booksellers or by contacting:
Level Head Publishing, LLC
Milwaukee, WI 53224

www.levelheadpublishing.com
levelheadpub@gmail.com

Dedication

For Him.

"The prophet that hath a dream, let him tell a dream;
and he that hath my word, let him speak my word faithfully."

Jeremiah 23:28

Acknowledgments

I would like to offer my sincere praise and thankfulness to the most important source in my life — God. Without Him and His Son in my life, I would have no spark or purpose. It is this same spark from Him that I see in others who are near and dear to me who have encouraged me and helped form the person I am today. So to all of my family and friends who find a piece of strength, an element of character, or even a wisecrack that reminds them of themselves in me — it's no mistake, and I thank you for sharing that part of "you" with "me". We build each other up in this lifetime, now look at what we have created! You've all played a role in this outcome…

Be Blessed!

CONTENTS

INTRODUCTION

Personally, if I were to pick up this book, I would probably wonder what was so funny about Jesus. Then I'd be relieved to see that there was nothing funny about Jesus and that it was just silly me who read the book cover wrong. But I'm positive that I would think there was something surely humorous about this author to have created such a title for this book. I mean, come on, *Jesus Is No Joke*? Is that even proper English? So, if I'm still playing me looking at my book from an outsider's perspective, I think I've got a couple of things right: This is a book that's not taking Jesus as a joke, yet some humor is involved.

Let's get back to being the real me, the one who actually wrote all of the stuff in this book. I can actually confirm my outsider assumptions to be true. This book is not a lot of talk where I slip in an unsuspecting "thus" or "thou" or make an attempt to talk over people's heads. I had always wished that someone would talk to me more casually about God and spiritual things without always keeping a straight face. So, I like to think of this book as a comfy Internet chat room where only my posts show up, but without all of the cursing of others popping up.

What's typical about this book on Jesus is, well... nothing. I haven't seen or heard of anyone truly try to talk "on the level" about Him where the average person could relate. Nor have I heard of anyone (other than me) with so little faith in Him talk about having actually seen Him — more than once. No, you didn't read that sentence wrong, I said (or wrote) that I have seen Him!

How do I explain such a thing happening to me? Well, that's what this book is all about, sharing my experiences and searching out answers for myself and (hopefully) for others. I wholeheartedly admit that God was always an acknowledged source in my life, but Jesus wasn't too huge on my scale of "knowing".

In the beginning of my encounters with Jesus, I was a science fiction fan who held UFO watches, drew comic strips, and attended an all-women's college while studying occupational therapy. I was plenty busy, had a ton of goals in my life, and rollerbladed until I dropped — when in popped Jesus!

If I were you reading this intro, the first thing I would think is, *Where did that fit in and how in the world can anyone be sure it is really Him or not?*

I wondered the same thing, but I now know there is no mystery to it. So many riddles that I thought I would never understand came into such clarity that now I cannot imagine life without knowing these things. It doesn't matter who you are, what you believe, what you have done, or where you live — Jesus is For Real.

He has always been here, always will be, and He will appear for all to see, someday. I know it may seem weird or odd to think of some flowing-robed being coming out of the sky to rid humanity of evil. At least *I* used to think that way. It all reminded me too much about Santa Claus, who would only reward the *good* boys and girls with presents at Christmas time.

I finally got over Santa's non-existence, as painful as that was, and if I could be made to believe in Santa, who was I to say that Jesus wasn't just another fantasy? There were too many similarities for me to ignore with this mesmerizing and rewarding nature that Santa and Jesus both possessed.

Now I realize that Jesus was the real character, better yet, Savior, which Christmas is based on. So real is He that I now sit here writing at a messy desk, stuttering in my mind about how

I can be sure to get the message out that this man named Jesus isn't just gossip or a Gospel tool. I can't think of any other way to gently get these points across, but to be who I am and write as I would talk to my friends. I'm telling this not to drive my story into anyone's brain to create converts, but to just put it out there for all to see one person's human approach to understanding what has happened to her. So I suggest that you tuck this book under your arm and head toward a comfy chair to peel back another page.

Consider this a personal story, where everyone could be the main character (who just so happened to be me this time around). There's a thought: Imagine it being you who saw Jesus and knew it to be true, against all odds. Could you keep it to yourself in fear of ridicule? Well, I've been made fun of for lesser things. So, I said to heck with it, and people with their little minds pointed to a thesaurus to find new words to describe "delusional".

This book is a conversation for the people I share this planet with who do have open minds!

For the record, I have no crowning authority over anything, either, so just because I wrote a book doesn't spell out "expert". Now, if you pull out the latest talk on the science fiction realm and aliens, then I would be a power to be reckoned with! So we won't go there.

For some reason, right now I feel like standing up in a group and saying, "My name is Heidi, and I saw Jesus." As if that would really help smack people with the impact and the magnitude of what that all really means. I just wish I could reach out and yank on people's eyelids to see what I have seen, so it wouldn't seem so strange or rare.

Hmm... perhaps someday I'll develop a virtual reality video game to do just that. For now, all I have is this book to pour my guts into. There's no fluff or fancy lettering I can add, either. Jesus is no joke, and my hope is that we can all realize this fact someday.

So watch out, here comes some talk on a Son who spoke of returning — and has.

1

WHERE WE ALL COME FROM

Jesus.

What do we think of that name when we say it, scream it, or moan it?

It's a name I'm sure we've all heard at one time or another. Whether some of us put much meaning into it or not, this name always seems to come up. I know that at one time, for myself, whenever I heard that name it felt like something old and distant. It was like this prehistoric figure who once was rumored to roam the land, never to be seen or heard from again.

At times imagery would pop into my head when I heard this name, which made it even harder to truly take in all that it meant. Sometimes I felt as if I were a little kid sitting around a campfire, eagerly leaning in as the elders would share stories passed down to them, "Yep, that Jesus fellow was somethin' else, He was! That bear stood anywhere between 10 and 15 feet tall! But Jesus didn't back down, no, sir! He stood His ground and gave that bear a good whacking upside his head! Ya better believe that bear went a-runnin'!"

Well, okay, maybe the images weren't *that* farfetched. Perhaps it was more like memories from childhood, where I was made to sit on hardwood church pews, shifting from one side to the other to allow blood to flow to my lower extremities. Then, at times, I'd have to pull my dress back down into place which had hiked up from all of the shifting, which would cause my pew-sticking skin to create audible screeching noises to be heard clear down the church rows. I'd usually look over in embarrassment to my sisters to see that they were doing practically the same thing, with an added whine and rolling of the eyes in "preaching-recipient" agony.

We were at church service, and there was no escape, we realized, but we were told we were supposed to be there, so we were. It still wasn't fun, not service sermons, anyway, but Sunday school was another story. We could handle the classes and actually tended to enjoy more of the one-on-one explanations instead of this mass address to an audience. I know I often wondered why the kids couldn't just end out their day with Sunday school and let the adults have their advanced classes in this more college-like forum.

But, nope.

We had to have our Sunday school, plus this hour of practicing to sit still — only to stand up when you saw everyone else do so. Not to mention bowing our heads in prayer, only to peek around to see if everyone was really closing their eyes when they tipped their heads forward and folded their hands. For the record, most people just seemed to be looking down at their laps or shoes. I could see the whites of their eyes at times, and that just doesn't happen if you truly have your eyes closed.

But, then, suddenly and mysteriously among all of the discomfort and spying, the pastor would heighten his voice in parts of his sentence to emphasize a name that would suddenly draw my eyes forward, "Jesus said . . . blah, blah, blah," only to lower his voice into something not memorable by a child.

So I'd heard the name Jesus before. I thought I knew where His place was in a book, too. The one that was written over, uh... well... a long time ago, called the Bible. Most people seem to be at least aware of the existence of the Bible, and I'm guessing that if they know it exists, they have at least opened it once or twice.

I admit that I'm not too savvy on the Bible, myself, but I did read a good deal of it some time ago. So bits and pieces of it have stuck in my head about the main points and ideas, I suppose. It seems to ring of "Be good, and don't let the darkness change you." But, of course, there's more to it than that, I realize. But to say that I have truly mastered the full details of the Bible would be far from the truth.

So, if someone thinks they can come up and out — quote me, you bet! But there's something to be said for where my heart is (It's just my head that can't always keep up with the quotes and reading and such.).

But back to Jesus: Who was, or is, this man, and where does He fit within our society? This is something I've often wondered.

I knew the general setting of the Bible: really ancient, lots of sand, with men and women walking around in big airy robes and sandals. There were kings, queens, empires, and lots of wars with hands-on battles with swords and rocks. Back in those days, people paid high taxes, and the amount of land you owned measured your wealth among your neighbors.

Scratch that last part, since those concepts have never changed.

But today things have changed quite a bit in considering this physical world. In today's playground, there are paved roads, dance clubs, televisions, cars, high schools, airplanes, technical gizmos, movies, and robotic pet dogs! These are just a few added distractions in this day and age to make it harder for the modern human to place how people in the Bible went about their daily lives. I doubt that many of us could even fathom having to wash our clothes by hand in our sinks, let alone go down to a river or well to beat our clothes with a rock. Envisioning those days of old is difficult enough, now try to manifest in your mind that God's Son Incarnate once traversed that very soil so long ago.

I'm trying to hold the thought, myself, and I think I have a decently assumed visual in my mind, since I have seen enough "Life of Jesus" specials on television. But to truly understand the whole concept of Jesus and what His life and sacrifice is about, can be a struggle to absorb.

I knew that a man by that name, claiming to be the Son of God, existed at one time. So for me it was pretty much historical fact, but I didn't know where He fit in with what I was doing today and if He was at all concerned with all of the atrocities which are going on in the world.

So, I suppose to quiet my own lack of answers where Jesus fit in, I just kept it out of my mind. I figured that if I didn't place judgment on it, how could I be for or against it? He had existed; I knew that, He performed miracles; I accepted that, and you had to say your prayers in His Name to get your point across to God.

Well, I knew all that, but this stuff was more memorized than personal. It was like there was more "head" stuff involved than "heart" when it came to Jesus.

For me, God was easy to know. I knew there was some higher being who started this whole earthen mystery. I feel that we are all born with this feeling that something or someone is missing in our lives, and we spend a great deal of our lifetime trying to find that missing piece. It's as if we came here with the distinct knowledge that part of our heart lies elsewhere and we need to reconnect to that "something else" to feel whole again. So we go where others are looking for that same missing piece — and it usually is in a worshiping place of one faith or another — and we try to piece the mystery together for ourselves. Someone, a long time ago, gave me a name for this pretty natural thing I personally felt and sought, and the name "God" stuck with me for the most part.

Now there goes another powerful name for you: God.

His is the very name we shout when we are in our most dire need, next to Jesus' name. Even if you didn't have faith before in

Him, suddenly it's the first thing out of your mouth when you're in trouble. Isn't that something?

I always thought that was one of the world's greatest mysteries. Here you have the rottenest of the rotten, sitting on death row, and suddenly he or she finds God. Surprisingly, now I understand more of that mystery.

People are essentially missing that link which I just mentioned, and we all realize it, no matter who we are. Most just don't have the patience to try to reconnect to it on a satisfactory level to feel secure and make that empty feeling go away. But sit a few years on death row, or feel like nothing can help you but a miracle, and you will surely make the time to throw out that light in you to form a rope to God to hoist you out of your situation.

Is that more of the miracle, that we find the time and means to call unto God only when needed, or did we know all along to truly mean it when we call out to Him to make things happen?

I know we all have it in us to make the connection whenever we want, but I think it's smart not to abuse it and to think that it can always be made up with one heartfelt call. Practice makes perfect. Keep your lifeline up and open so maintenance will be minimal when you need to make a call. Now I feel like a long-distance phone service, but the concept was so similar that I couldn't help myself.

I'm the first to admit that I am no angel in anyone's eyes. At times, I'm just as guilty as the next person, especially when it comes to slacking on the prayer end. But I have learned to make communication with God easier for myself by not placing so many restrictions on myself in the manner in which I can speak with Him. So, when it comes to God, I feel great about where I stand with Him for a variety of reasons which I'll mention later.

But Jesus? Was it really necessary that I know and fully understand what was meant by Him and His actions, even today? I figured I had the God thing down pretty good, so there was no need to dig any further, just go by memory on how to address God through Jesus, and all would be fine.

Well, today I'm inclined to say that it was not a wise decision, because it could have cost me dearly in more ways than I can count. I also would have spread my arrogance and ignorance to others and been partly responsible for their deception. I suppose (Well, there is no "supposing" to it, really.) I know that God saw that I was a decent person who was making an awful mistake. So, what better way to help me see the light than to wake me up personally with a special visitor?

There's no mystery about who I'm speaking of, unless you missed all the name-dropping going on. There is no way in my wildest dreams that I could surmise I would ever meet Jesus, but then again, I don't know why I thought it could *never* be possible. The conflicting thoughts which a mind can give you are something else. That's why I feel it's best to go with one's heart on most things.

But, yes, *I saw Jesus!* Not just once or twice, either.

When I say it aloud, or write it down, it sounds wild even to me. It just seems too grand to have happened to me — or to anyone else, for that matter. But when I think back on how His Presence felt and all of the emotions I have attached to my encounters with Him, it's not hard for me to be assured and not care how wild it sounds to say it.

I know what my life experiences have been and what I've seen. In all honesty, I'm not concerned how my experiences may be perceived by outsiders on their grading scale of how Jesus encounters should be presented.

It's funny how some may try to place limits on God and Jesus, Who most believers admit as having limitless powers. They might say, "Oh, but that can't happen that way! Because evil can come as an angel of light, as it's quoted in the Bible."

Rationalizing if evil prevailed by making appearances as something positive should help clear an outsider's perspective to another about an apparently holy visitor.

I like to use my common sense to explain that I doubt the devil would come to me just so I could talk about Jesus and God to a few more people. But to argue for or against any of this is not my issue.

I'm just here to share what has come my way in hopes that it will inspire others who think Jesus is some ancient Son of God who once came, never to stop by since. There's much to know about Him and His ongoing Work, and I don't pretend to have all of the answers. Yet, if I can open up my life and encounters to give even a hint more about Jesus, then I'm more than honored to be an instrument to help out.

CHAPTER

2

WHERE I'M COMING FROM

~Tidbit: What an in-depth chapter this one's going to be! There's almost too much to mention about my assorted background, which brought me to where I am today, that I know I won't be able to relate here. In fact, parts of my background are so diverse that it might not even be perceived as relatable to the topic at hand. All I can say is that I'll do my best to keep my focus while looking down the line of my life, so I won't stray too far off the subject. ~

What most people would call strange occurrences have always been a part of my life. Since I was a kid, I guess you could say my two sisters and I were a bit gifted in experiencing things that most people did not. I didn't always think it was called a gift
— more like haunted. Well, the house we lived in was haunted anyway, and it wasn't anything fun, either.

My mother passed away when I was seven years old, and she'd lived in our home for about five years, from the time we moved back to Milwaukee from San Francisco. My folks were at odds with each other and nearing a divorce when my mother suffered a heart attack while driving, which caused her to steer off the road and into a building. My mom had nine children in total. I tell people it took that many kids for her to get it right so I could be born, since I was baby number eight. I figure that God must have told her I was coming. Now watch my siblings give me head noogies for saying that one, but it's a risk I must take. ☺

Odd things started to happen in our house that first Christmas Day following my mom's passing. Things moved on their own, toys played by themselves, screwed-shut attic doors suddenly dropped open, loud knockings were heard, presences were felt, and on at least two occasions something ghostly was seen.

I was the middle child of this generation of two other siblings (I had six older siblings who'd already moved out of the house.) and a soon-to-be stepbrother. When the odd things started to happen I was eight years old, so one can imagine that I hardly found this haunted house situation amusing, in fact, I was scared out of my wits!

Some have told me that because of the timing, it must have been my mother haunting the house, angry that my father had moved on with his life. But, as I mentioned, they were nearing a divorce anyway, so that line had already been drawn and decided upon between the two of them. Aside from that, to imagine that my mother would involve her own kids in the haunting process made no sense, either. I like to think that when she was alive, she kept whatever presence it was at bay, but when she passed, there was less protection to keep this haunting force out.

I'd later learn more on what was truly coming our way as kids, because these odd and terrible things would rear their ugly heads throughout my life. These things were shapeless shadowy things, which I later called "Shadow People" only to learn to call them "Shadows" later in life (That whole story about them is literally another book.). To put it in a nutshell, darkness is darkness, and it began to come when some of the light in the house went away with my mom's passing. No, she wasn't a perfectly easy-going person, but there was always that innate protectiveness a mother has for her children — and that's called love. With love there's light, and dark presences are not too keen on that love thing.

My new stepmother, my dad, and we four kids finally moved to a house my parents had constructed on a plot of land that had once been an apple and pear tree orchard. That suited us kids just fine, since several of the fruit trees still remained, so we often indulged in the fruit when it was in season. I was suspicious that we had moved to a newly built house partly because there was less risk of there being any ghosts in the house. I'll also confess that my suspicions are due to my stepmom mentioning that it was indeed part of her reasoning, although not fully.

The haunting issue went right out the window, for the most part, once we moved. It was that or we just refused to think anything out of the ordinary could or would happen any longer.

Things had changed where objects didn't move on their own and such, except for one time when a vase somehow got thrown across the room when I was the only one home. It wasn't me, but I was held responsible and had to replace that darn vase. I can now understand that it was an odd thing to believe that anything strange would happen in this newly built home. But heck, I like to keep bringing it up anyway to let the guilt sink in for my folks, since they didn't believe me at the time.

Even before that one poltergeist incident happened, soon after we moved in, a new set of experiences started happening on a different level. Odd dreams, horrid ones that used images of my deceased mother, started to creep into my mind at night. That would be interesting in an odd way if those dreams were unique, but they weren't. My two sisters and I were all having the same theme in our dreams!

It took some time for us to realize that we shared those dreams, because those dreams did not represent our mother in a very positive view. It's nothing that I truly care to repeat in detail here, only to say that they were dark, violent, and nearly always with an evil, paranormal twist (nothing that could or did happen in real life). For me, those dreams repeated a few times but were mostly changing and went on from the age of 9 until I was 24 or more.

The haunting and scary dreams were only one end of the spectrum of rare events in my life. In all honesty, they didn't seem so rare, since these were shared occurrences in my family. In fact, my siblings and I found peace in watching horror movies just to see how movie characters dealt with their terror.

Back then, a movie just wasn't a movie if it wasn't scary, where I could apply some psychology and reasoning to them. When I would watch the movies with my siblings, we would rate the actions of the characters to see if they did the right thing or not. It was like, "No, no, no! This is where you run man — RUN!" and, "Sis, when that happened to you, didn't you lock yourself in the bathroom?" or, "Ghosts can't do that!" Then there's, "Spinning head? I guess we were lucky that one didn't happen!"

Terror had made its mark on us for certain, but as I said, it was only one end of the spectrum for me. From as early as I can remember, I also had lucid dreams and visions of being in a Heaven-like place and being spoken to by angelic beings in white, flowing gowns. Much like the dreams of my mother, these heavenly "dreams" were so real that it was hard to believe they did not actually occur. I called these positive and influential dreams and visions "waking dreams".

It's hard to recall them all, but some were so intense that they are not easily forgotten. These waking dreams are moving and full of messages, with so much detail and imagery that I know I don't have the imagination to have created them on my own. For lack of a better way to communicate how impacting these waking dreams can be, I'll share one I still hold onto, so many years later:

One of my most moving waking dreams happened when I was about 17 years old. I suddenly found myself being guided by a man whose face I cannot recall outright. He wore a white, flowing gown that reached the ground where I could not see his feet.

11

I remember glancing intently at his gown as he stood only a few feet away from me. When he put out his hands as if to present something, that's when I looked around to see that I was standing on the outskirts of what I now call the "Crystal City". Off in the distance I could see magnificent structures in a city made up entirely of crystals and sparkling marble. A brilliant, pure-white glow emitted from the city, which felt as cozy as a village nestled in a valley.

My gowned guide and I then began to walk toward the city, and as we came closer to the buildings, I could see that they looked much like ancient Roman buildings with fancy pillars and trim. The first thing I recall doing was walking up to one of the pillars and placing my right hand on the opposite side of the pillar. With the dazzling spectacle of seeing crystal pillars, I wanted to know if I could actually see my hand through the pillar on the other side.

There were sparkling, dancing lights in the crystal pillar, and it had a very slight hint of blue when I walked up closer to it. It reminded me of a sparkling gel, and the lights were so dense in the pillar that it made it hard to see my hand on the other side. I could still make it out ever so slightly, and I found this amusing that I could make out my hand but could not see what was on the interior of the buildings made of the same crystal, although denser.

The guide I was with then walked me past other structures in this crystal collage of wondrous buildings, although several of the buildings appeared to be made of a sparkling-white marble upon closer inspection. I saw people like myself lined up outside one building waiting to walk into a visible doorway. Some of the people had regular clothes on, but most had on white gowns, just like my guide. I don't recall what I was wearing or truly care about it either, but when I think back on it today, I feel I might have been in a white gown as well.

I asked my guide if I was to stand in line with the people, and he said no. He then walked me down what I can call a yard, with walking paths that had a wonderful cloud of mist which hung low over the surface. We stopped when we were in front of a large building that seemed taller than the others we had passed. This building also had an interesting yard or garden in front of it, unlike anything I'd seen in front of the others.

The garden was small and close to the front of the building, and it had narrow, paved paths that led up to a pedestal. The pedestal had a thin pillar that came to just above my waist, and there was a scroll laid on top of it like an open book, and both were made of an almost marble-like stone.

My guide stood at a comfortable distance from me, as if to allow me to investigate my surroundings freely.

As I leaned in closer, I read several names that were etched on the scroll. I wish I could recall which names were there but some details often escape me when I'm on excursions of this sort. As I continued to read the names to myself, I looked up at my guide and asked him if my name was on the scroll. I don't know why I thought to ask such a thing, but for some reason the question came from me.

The guide said, "No, but soon it will be."

He then walked toward me and put out his hand to guide me to the opening of the large building we were standing in front of. I walked in, and my guide remained standing near the doorway. Almost as if I knew my place and where to go, my eyes stayed focused to the front of this single large room inside the building. I then walked right up to the front row of some horseshoe-shaped bleacher seats. The seats seemed to be carved from the stone that made up the flooring of this building, and I found my "known" place and promptly sat down.

There was an instructor lecturing to a class. However, I could not see anyone else, or perhaps I was simply so mesmerized by what was being said that I didn't bother to take notice of the others. Whatever was being disclosed by this instructor in a white flowing robe, I was so engulfed and attuned to it that when I sat down in my place on the seating, I just meshed with the others who sat silently, taking mental notes.

I have since had several memories and/or waking dreams of being in this Heaven-like place. I also recall being with other angelic people in white robes who have guided me through this Heaven-place and have even appeared to me in person as varying shapes of light, often in the shape of spheres. The spheres were different, of course, in appearance from the robed people. But their "feel" was the same, so I knew it to be them and others who worked for God.

I understand that some might think that a person who has something like a waking dream is just simply dreaming or that an occasional encounter with angelic beings is just the eyes playing tricks. Something to consider is how so much content of the Bible is based on dreams and angelic messengers or protectors. We still take the word of these people and their dreams centuries later, but, today, should we discount and disregard our dreams as if no message of truth can be presented in them? Pardon me for saying so, but I do find that to be awfully strange and sightless on our part if we would disregard such things.

I can say that I'm not one to ignore what comes to me at night. I believe there's a reason why our body needs to shut down and that much of it has to do with our needing to recharge our soul just as much as our body. Something I've often wondered is, *Where does all this me go when I sleep?*

I doubt that my soul just lies there trying to think up things to entertain itself. A crystal city and white-robed beings are a bit of a stretch for most anyone to create on their own. I'm certain that our worries from day to day intervene much of the time in our dreams, but that is not the sole source of our dream content. I think most of us know ourselves and what we like, what our interests are, what's on our minds, what we would like to do with ourselves or situations, and so on.

People draw from where they've been and what they've experienced, so the chances of coincidentally and continually envisioning a solid city with angelic beings is quite slim. I've now heard of several stories from others who speak of visiting this Crystal City, including the writings of Enoch, who is considered by some as the first prophet and is written of in the Bible.

I'm no prophet. I'm too ordinary for all that, but I'm darned glad that I'm not the only one, even alive today, who has seen this city. Being in the presence of the white-robed beings is also something I could not even fathom to duplicate where they have this thick ribbon of love spiraling from them.

Sometimes when I awake in my bed, I feel as if I've spent some time with these spiritual beings, but I do not outright recall what took place. I often just wake up with this feeling of having received a download of warm packets of information which reside just at the tip of my mind. It can be frustrating at times to feel there's something that I want to remember, but I know when that happens that it's just not its time to be recalled. But the essence of love in the air tells me all I need to know, that they were there and that what was taught to me is in my heart.

It seems that when I was surrounded by darkness or negativity the most is when these angelic presences increased, as if to protect me. At times, I could feel or even see shadowy presences coming my way in the night, only to have a positive presence in the form of various lights come to protect me. The intrusions of darkness reminded me of my childhood, being taunted by unseen forces in my haunted home.

It didn't matter where I would move, darkness seemed to follow me, but the light was even closer. It felt like there was a battle at hand, and in this front I was the one being impressed upon. From childhood until adulthood, evil made its presence known, but it could never win. Had I not welcomed the positive, the negative might have made its impression upon me stick a bit better.

15

There's always a choice to be made, and I am happy that I made the right one — to remain open to the lighter side of things. Had I not opened my heart, I'm certain Jesus would not have seen an invitation to appear. I think for anyone that it's wise to make the effort to know what Jesus is about. It's even wiser to open the door before He knocks.

Believe it or not, I was not the wisest when it came to doors. While I was writing my first book called *The Secret War*, I dared to make a bold statement that I later ate in reconciliation. I had seen so many strange things and white-robed, angelic beings that I actually wrote, "If Jesus were around, I would have seen Him by now."

What made me so cocky, I cannot tell you. What it does go to show you is that no one can stand on this green Earth and say they have seen it all! I truly thought I had, but I had hardly gotten started.

There was one story in particular that stuck in my mind the most, when it came to stories of this "seeing Jesus" sort, which was of Betty Jean Eadie and her book *Embraced by the Light*. I recall standing in a local bookstore, fingering through the pages and reading her words about a near-death experience she had and what she saw on the other side. She even spoke about seeing life spread across the galaxy on many planets and how she felt she had to return here to Earth to spread God's Word.

All that was mentioned in her book was fine and dandy with me, but when I came across her saying that she had met Jesus, I believe I rolled my eyes and totally chalked up her experience to misinterpretation. I did believe that she believed she had seen and experienced all that she mentioned, don't get me wrong. But as I mentioned, I somehow had this superior notion that since I'd seen so much unearthly stuff already in my brief lifetime, Jesus would have surfaced at some point.

Yes, I know I had some nerve. Yet, I truly thought that Eadie just assumed one of those white-robed beings she saw was Jesus.

Heck, it fit the profile, but I'd seen beings like this, too, and I knew they weren't Jesus. I felt so strongly about such misconceptions of this sort that I made it a point to use visions of Jesus as an example in my first book for seeing things that are not what they appear to be.

I mean it; I actually did write that chapter, and you'd better believe I rewrote it when I came to my senses later on, too! In this chapter, I had used comparisons of Jesus sightings to how people might see animal shapes in the clouds. I called the chapter, "Supposed Evidence vs. True Insight: What's Real?" Oh, I was good, I totally endorsed that people were drawing conclusions and placing titles to something they knew nothing of.

Boy! Was I wrong!

The funny part of it all is that the "powers that be" knew I was wrong, too, and decided to let me off the hook. Besides, there was a sure chance that I might influence others with my misleading words on printed pages, which for some makes it seem like gospel since it's published. But writers are wrong all the time. We have opinions just like anyone else, and I just cringe at the thought that I almost messed up big time.

I'm happy to say that messing up wasn't meant to be. I was one of the lucky ones who had a special visitor come by and straighten me out. That visitor altered my tune and left me forever changed. Thank God!

CHAPTER

3

SPEAKING OF GOD . . .

~Tidbit: I was just debating with myself if I should write more on how God has been in my life or just skip ahead to my Jesus encounters. It took all of 30 seconds for me to think, "Duh!" Of course I would have to speak about God. Heck, I'm talking about His Son, so how in the world could I skip around that? I don't know how my brain works at times, but, yeah, back to God!~

Well, He has never let me down, I can say that much. Whenever I've felt like all is lost, I swear, just the most unbelievable things would happen that have picked me up right out of my situation. Sometimes that's been literally where I've been picked right up, too. I'll explain in more detail, but I want to say that I've chosen to share this story because it truly is one of my first most profound recollections of God's interventions.

As a teen, I lived a good distance away from public transportation. For the most part, to get anywhere I had to walk, bike, or roller skate, and I did it all. My folks weren't too generous on the car rides with four teenage kids at home all wanting to go places — and surely not to my part-time job at McDonald's.

It was about a two-mile walk to the nearest bus stop to get to my job, and if I didn't have bus money, I'd just walk the entire distance with an added mile on top of it. So I braved it all and trudged through whatever came my way. There were tons of times where I would be quite angry that my folks wouldn't give me a ride in just simply horrible weather conditions, but I did what I felt I had to do.

I lived in Wisconsin, and still do, and to anyone who doesn't know about winters here, I suggest driving around the state during that time. Find a different route, or, if you insist, pack things like blankets and emergency equipment in your trunk for the unexpected car freezing or failure. It just isn't pretty, the cold that is. Winter is nice to look at from your window, but I'd prefer to look at it from a postcard as I vacation in Puerto Rico or somewhere.

Anyway, during my regular winter back-and-forth hikes of two miles or more each way, I'd often feel desperate. Not too many cars traveled the roads where I lived, nor were there many streetlights or sidewalks to walk on, for that matter. So I'd walk on the side of the road, often in fear when a car would go by. Sometimes cars drove by too slowly, and I'd pick up my pace with a little bounce to appear to be a guy walking along, instead of a frightened teenage girl. When I was especially scared, I'd run the whole distance, and even faster over a bridge where I heard rumors of horrible people hanging around there. Needless to say, my athletic abilities were enhanced from these long-distance runs, and I put that to good use by joining every sport there was at my high school.

Traversing the ground with no barriers was an effort, but to do so with several feet of snow on the ground, with below zero winds whipping by, that was even harsher. Even before thinking of having to go out in weather like that, I would feel depressed and helpless that I had no other way to get to where I needed to go. So, when I was in the middle of actually walking through the snow, especially at night, my anxiety only worsened. I would constantly be talking to myself to push on, coaching myself that I could do it and make it home safely. But sometimes those walks were just too long, the wind was too cold, and the snow too deep.

I would occasionally stop and look around and feel so alone. No one really knew where I was, and it felt that no one really cared, for that matter, on these long walks there and back. There were several times when my entire body went numb and my face was chapped with eye and nose drippings frozen to my face, which made my misery grow to unbearable heights.

One night, in near white-out conditions and below freezing temperatures, I thought to myself, *I can't move anymore.* My body had come to a slow, cold, halt — like a battery losing its charge. I literally felt like I was on the verge of dying out there, freezing to death, and with no way to get help. It's hard to describe such dread, desperation, and then a wilting feeling for my very life. I started to weigh my options, as I looked toward the woods just off the roadside, thinking that I should try to crawl toward them to let God take my soul from there. That way I figured I wouldn't be an eyesore on the roadside in the morning for any drivers on their commute to work.

But then I got an idea and thought to pray. I don't know why trying to figure where to plop my frozen body down to die came to mind first, but at least prayer came in at some point. I usually was quicker to pray while I did anything that was tough, but in my most desperate time on this walk, I was too down to even think about it until I realized death might be a reality. That's a typical human response, eh?

So I sputtered out a weak prayer. I didn't have much else left in me to say, aside from, "Help me, God."

At that moment, I was stopped dead in the snow, partially on my knees, bent over, leaning to one side, and trying to catch my breath. My hair was tucked into a Green Bay Packers hat and my body was sorely disfigured in a bulky coat and mismatched gloves.

At the most, a minute passed by with no answer to my prayer, and hope slipped from me. That's when I heard his voice.

"Heidi? Is that you?"

Well, I knew it wasn't God literally talking! I remember slowly turning around, only to look into the face of a guy from one of my high school classes. He was sitting in his blue Trans-Am, leaning out his window. "Do you need a ride somewhere?" he asked.

The wind was so loud, the snow was so heavy, and I was so frozen that I hadn't even heard his car pull up! I could scarcely focus to make out who was talking to me, because I barely knew this guy (I'd hardly ever spoken to him.). I figured it was safe since he knew who I was, obviously, so I piled into his car.

I honestly don't recall being able to speak too much, except to point out where I lived, but I remember the guy standing outside his car watching with concern as I frozenly staggered to the front door of my house. I was speechless and still frozen upon entering my parent's home and went directly to my bedroom to thaw out.

I remember bunching myself around my bedroom heater in agony, and it felt like my fingers and toes would explode as warm blood made its way through my extremities. The pain was of little matter, as I was still stunned and thankful that God had actually heard my cries. It was such a purposeful and immediate response that there was just no other explanation for what had taken place.

As I mentioned, there were other incidences very similar to this one on the same stretch of road, and whenever I was at the end of my strength, someone came out of the blue and picked me up in their car. These weren't strangers who came by either, because I knew better than to just get into a car with anyone. But how these people could recognize me in my bunchy winter clothes, while they sped through the blowing snow and darkness, I'll never know.

This all just blew my mind, to say the least. But it was a sure sign for me to truly see that God was in my life and was seeing to it that I was safe. My anxiety of walking in the snow nearly dissipated after this first incident, because I somehow just knew I could call on Him for help if I felt I couldn't go on any longer.

You know what? God never failed me. Not once. I took salvation in knowing that He was watching and always near. I also got the strong feeling that I was going to be sticking around for some time to do tasks in my life to somehow help His cause, too. But that feeling wasn't so new, it was something that was an integral part of me early on. There was just a "knowing" I had in me about some purpose, so it all didn't just start after my cold winter walks.

The earliest recollection I have of this awareness started with a specific incident when I was about six years old.

The day started off like any other, except for the sinking reality that I would have to go to church that day. As a kid, it wasn't like, "Yippee! I get to go and learn more about God." It was more like, "Oh great, it's not even a school day, and I have to get up early just to listen to another adult teach me something they think is important."

Throughout most of my childhood, I don't know what was worse, the teaching part or getting up early. I think the getting up early part outweighed most of it, though, since I've never been an early riser.

The day started off with my digging through my closet trying to find something that wasn't jeans or a skirt, but neutral. Then I found a pair of slacks that had the fewest wrinkles and slapped them on with some kind of matching blouse. I got the usual curious look from my folks, who then asked why I never chose to wear a dress, and I then redirected my choice of clothes to some drab dress hidden in my closet.

I was reasonably into wearing the frilly dresses of my time, but I did mention that I was raised in Wisconsin, didn't I? Winter seems to last just a bit longer in my neck of the woods, and dresses don't come to my mind around that time. Yet, after my folks redirected me, I donned a dress in agony and muttered under my breath about having to wear something I didn't want to and go to a place my parents themselves rarely went to.

My folks would just drop us kids off, seeing to it that we were enlightened. It was that or they just wanted to have the day to themselves. My logical side says they truly wanted us kids to be closer to God, but now that I'm an adult, I see it was a mini-vacation day for them, too. Either way, I'm glad I got some hint of spiritual guidance early on in my life.

Unknowingly, on this one particular Sunday, I truly was about to get tapped into my more spiritual side and react to it stronger than I could ever have imagined while being a reluctant but adventurous kid.

My Sunday school teacher was a younger woman in her mid-thirties, the friendly sort who kept our teachings lively and fun. But she had something specially planned for us on this day. She was going to talk to us for the first time about the Book in the Bible called *Revelations.*

She talked in a quiet, more reserved voice and spoke of how God promised to take away what was bad on the Earth and make things right. As she spoke, I remember listening with my ears but feeling it more with my heart. It hurt, but then there was joy inside of me, knowing of the new beginning that awaited those who were faithful to God. A tear slowly curled in the corner of my eye, and I quickly wiped it away.

Afterward, I went to the church sermon kind of mystified and secretly embarrassed about my emotional response to what had been taught earlier that day in class. I was an embarrassed six-year -old; does that ever happen? My mind was busy contemplating so much that I hardly regarded where I was sitting, which made the sermon service fly by quickly, much to my delight.

That evening, when my dad was tucking me into bed for the night, all of my emotions and thoughts from the day flowed forward. I started crying, and my dad asked, with concern, what was the matter. I told him what my Sunday school teacher had taught us about the days of Revelations and how so many horrible things were going to happen. I remember my dad smiling at me and saying how there was nothing to worry about, because all of that was so far in the future.

Well, that explanation didn't help the matter of my personal revelation about Revelations! The tears in my eyes didn't subside, as I sobbed to my dad and said, "I'm gonna be living then."

He seemed a little surprised over this remark from such a little person, and I quickly sat up in bed to get a hug from my dad. He calmed me, told me to get some sleep, and not to worry anymore.

A six-year-old talking about living during the end of the world? What a strange thing.

In my heart of hearts, the mentioning of "end times" somehow had a ring of familiarity and truth for me. At the time, I hardly knew what I was saying when I said this to my dad, but there was something in me that knew something that I didn't know I knew (if that makes sense). I'd always had a stranger than usual perspective on life and things around me as a kid. I just seemed to pay attention to things out of the ordinary and inquired about them.

To have a differing angle in perspective is one thing, but this was my heart that was somehow "in the know" crying out to me.

Ever since I had that revelation, I suppose one could say I realized there was a part of me that was hidden from my direct view. Yet, it was not until something came along and triggered a reaction in me that I would get hints and clues which I was to follow and trust.

Trusting was, and still sometimes is, a huge factor in getting to know this mysterious-yet-spiritual side of me and what comes my way. As with those tears which I shed about Revelations, I had no backup or proof why I felt I would be around for the end times. I wondered a lot about my understanding of this, other occurrences, where these odd notions came from, and why they would come as they did and not at another time. It simply was and is not easy to trust some spontaneous feeling coming out of nowhere like that. I couldn't see any direct use for any of it, and I surely wasn't going to voice any of this in public as if I were some kind of seer or psychic.

Thank goodness I was not always having things pop up in my psyche like that. Heck, I would never have been able to concentrate on the "here and now" if I had. I doubt I'd look very sane, either, or mistakenly gain a guru-like status if I did fully go all out with all of this. I figure that this life has enough roller-coaster thrills already than to add that on top of it.

So, yeah, God and elements surrounding the topic of Him were no small element in my life, early on, but it was also something I didn't know what to do with for quite a while, even well into my early adulthood. As a teen, I felt that if I didn't dwell on any of the insightful-spiritual feelings I had coming my way, they would quiet down. Being a teen was an awkward period on its own, so I surely didn't want to bring more confusion to my situation. However, I also didn't feel I had to fully allow myself to be pulled in a manner I was uncomfortable with, no matter the topic at hand.

In the beginning of my teen years, the time was ripe for me to be committed, or, rather, confirmed, to my church by taking confirmation classes on Thursday nights. I started with the classes, which was attended by my regular friends at Sunday school, so it was comfortable at first. But something inside of me wanted to get some answers first about my having seen and understanding things a bit out of the norm before I could allow myself to be fully committed to any church.

I was a bit on the shy side then, so after a regular Sunday school class, I approached my teacher, who was also an ordained minister. I asked him about people who claimed to know parts of the future and see things that most people didn't see. I made the question pretty vague, not wanting to draw attention to myself, because I didn't want to be exorcised or anything.

I remember him stopping, turning around, and saying to me in a matter-of-fact manner, "Why, only God knows the future, but only the devil will try and tell it with deceit. So if a person is receiving anything, it must be from the devil, and they are possessed, because *God* won't tell it."

It seemed that he just left out the part about seeing things many don't, but his words stopped me dead in my tracks. He was saying that I was evil and in touch with evil things.

I don't feel evil, I thought to myself. *If that's the way this church feels about people like me, then it's not for me. Something is missing here.*

I decided right then, at the age of 13, that I was not going to commit myself to this church and what it represented, because it didn't represent who I was. I was tremendously insulted — but secretly. I did share it with one of my sisters, though, who also seemed to take offense, since she and I had these similar abilities.

I thought it was very closed-minded for anyone to take the stance which my supposed "spiritual mentor" had. Now as an adult, I think I know who he may have been referring to. Most likely he was thinking of the commercialized, flowing-gowned psychics who were trying to make a buck on an assumed talent, peering into a crystal ball while irresponsibly and/or purposefully misleading people. I know that not all psychics do this, but it's the commonly perceived notion, no matter how stereotyped that imagery is.

But I wasn't any of this; I was a teenage girl looking for some answers. Although he didn't know it, his answer shattered me.

I'd always complied with my parents' wishes about most things they wanted from me. I didn't try to be difficult. But when it came to my going to Thursday night confirmation classes, after that discussion with my teacher, I put my foot down. I told my parents that I didn't want to get confirmed, but I got dropped off for the class anyway. Yes, church was one of the few places my folks would at times drive me to. Whether they were fully aware or not, I refused to go into the class. I would stand outside the whole time, and I didn't care how cold it was.

My parents would pull up, and I'd be in the same spot where they had dropped me off, and I'd have nothing to say about how things were coming along. I couldn't make it up, and I wouldn't; I simply was not present.

I suppose that parental intuition told them something, because, on their own, they stopped bringing it up and taking me to the class. I didn't mind one bit, but for some reason I still got a specially signed Bible addressed to me as if I'd finished the class. It was given to me after the others went through their confirmation ceremony, so they somehow felt it necessary to include me to get my Bible. I don't know how that worked out, but I still have it today, around here *somewhere*.

As a whole, from that time forth, I did stray away from the controlled belief systems set up in churches. I never gave up my faith; I just gave up following what another person said was the path to God and followed my own heart to God. My body was my temple, or so I had been taught, and that's where I worshiped — in my heart. I felt that as long as I kept true in my heart on how I felt about God, without trying to prove anything to anyone, then I would be fine.

For the most part, I felt I truly was a good, decent, and honest person. I liked to help people just because it brought me joy, and that was my reward. I didn't curse until I was 19; I never much liked drinking, was faithful in my relationships, and always looked for the good in people and in situations.

Somehow, though, I still truly lacked the understanding of what Jesus was all about. I didn't think it was that big of a deal to remain in my ignorance. I felt that as long as I was okay with God, then it was okay to be confused about Jesus.

Now I know better; there was nothing okay about it. Things needed to be righted if I were to truly understand God as He should be. Being just "okay" about anything with God doesn't make the cut. Being able to say I am "great" with God sounds and feels a whole lot better!

CHAPTER

4

JESUS (OR HAY-SOOS)?

July 19th, 1999 was a day like any other. I worked part-time at a local grocery store, usually from 6:00 A.M. until 12:00 noon. Being a night person, I could never bring myself to get to bed much sooner than midnight. So, generally, I would come home from work just a wee bit tired and looking forward to a nice afternoon nap before I continued my day.

Still fresh on my mind from a couple of weeks earlier was a July 4th cookout at my sister Wanda's house, where I'd had an absolute blast! There was lots of food to be had with the grill lit up, various salads for every fancy, and sweets to back it all up! Four of my sisters, along with nephews, nieces, and tons of friends, all came together to enjoy the celebration of our country's Independence Day.

After a few rounds of indulging on snacks and goodies, I joined my sister, Keisha, and my niece in toying around with a basketball behind Wanda's house. We were all wearing sandals and somewhat dressed up, so we weren't taking anything too seriously in making our shots through the hoop.

But then a challenge came our way. Quincy, a friend of our family, along with my nephew, Robert, and his best friend, decided they couldn't sit idly by and watch us innocent young ladies on the court any longer. I believe Quincy was the first to make a challenging statement, saying something along the lines that we didn't have a prayer against them.

The next thing I knew, our sandals came off, then we pulled our hair back and leaned forward. My sister, Keisha, was wearing a dress with heels. She quickly whipped those shoes off and prepared to stand her ground. She hiked up her dress and partially wrapped it around her thighs with a knot and motioned for the boys to bring it on!

Most people know of the Williams sisters being an unbeatable pair when it comes to playing doubles in tennis. Well, little did we know the Hollis sisters (and niece) were comparable in basketball! We'd never tested our skills quite like that, aside from our high school days, and we were apparently overdue.

To sum it up nicely, we whooped the tar out of those guys and heard cries from them being "gentlemen" and that's why they had lost. Whether that was the case or not, they declared they wanted a rematch, which made me think they'd be less gentlemen-like to prove their point for the next game.

With the festivities of the day coming to a close and some folks needing to get home, we didn't have time for a rematch, unfortunately, but we indeed planned on doing so. I especially was eager to put Quincy in check with all of the "crap talking" he was doing throughout the game, all in good fun, of course. So a rematch sounded much to my liking, and I truly hoped that day would come.

Two weeks later, the joy of that day was still not easily forgotten, as I came home from work to take my afternoon nap. I got home around 12:15 P.M. and waved to my roommate to turn down her television so I could get my usual shuteye. I then walked into my bedroom, closed the door behind me, and quickly reached for the rod to twist my shades closed to block out the afternoon sunlight. I kicked off my shoes, smoothed out my blankets, and spun my legs around on top of the covers. I nudged a little at my pillow and leaned back with a smile to count down my moment of pillow impact . . . 3 . . . 2 . . . 1 . . .

Where am I!? I wondered, as I looked around in this familiar scene.

I felt that I had just placed my head on my pillow only to fall through it and land in some sort of vivid scenery. This rapid transition from my bedroom to this place happened so quickly that it surprised and puzzled me, even had it only been the onset of a mere dream! I've never been one to nod off and go to sleep immediately; there's always some moving about to get comfy and tossing thoughts of daily events out of my head. I tried to justify to myself that I must have been more tired than I thought, or there was something else going on that the puzzling effect even met me in my "dream". However, I soon discovered that this was no dream, but the beginning of something much more spectacular!

There was something familiar about the place in which I found myself, although it looked a little different. I was right next to my parents' home. For some reason, a lot of waking dreams and other visions I have had (that even included my mother) seemed to take place in front of my folks' home. Perhaps there's some underlying reason for this, but I'm never really puzzled as to why I'm at my parents' home, even though I don't get to see my folks that often. But in this "dream" I was a bit mystified about my being at my parents' home, and I was standing near some dumpsters next to their house — dumpsters that are not actually there in real life, which puzzled me even more.

So, I'm standing there in this fenced-in dumpster area connected to the side of my parents' home, wondering why I'm there, when I saw a man walking my way off in the misty distance. By the size and stature of the man, he looked much like our family friend, Quincy, so I tried to rationalize to myself that I must be at my folks' house for that basketball rematch we planned on. I had so much fun that day. I was really looking forward to getting the chance to hang out with family and friends, which seemed to happen only when holidays came.

The man continued to approach me walking through misty clouds that seemed to hang low to the surface of the ground he walked on. As the man got closer to me, something inside me told me that my perception was way wrong. A tickling sensation in my stomach began to resonate, and I put my face in my hands in disbelief as he approached, and my realization grew stronger. I felt silly somehow, and at the time, placing my face in my hands was my usual manner when I was in disbelief or got stumped on something, not that I'm silly any longer (Look at that, I could hardly keep a straight face even typing that just now.). Okay, so it's something I still might do if I feel the urge. It's kind of like the smack to the forehead you see done in cartoons, but that would hurt too much, so my face in my hands works better for me.

So, again, there I stood, near some non-existent dumpsters, when this man finally reached me and walked into the fenced area. His halt was with ease, as he stopped to begin to speak with me.

"Hello," the man said in a friendly sort of way, almost as if he were going to talk about the weather in the next sentence.

I still had my head down, was rubbing my forehead, and slightly looking his way, when I responded with an equally friendly, "Hello."

I stood there thinking over and over in my head, *This isn't happening; this just can't be who I think it is.*

I know my mannerism was somewhat childish, and I don't think the man took offense, but with a kidding yet urgent tone he called my bluff on my reactions.

My eyes were still covered with one hand, but I felt him lean my way ever so slightly and ask, "Do you know who I am?"

My heart was quivering in my chest now, as it battled my mind in allowing what was evident to be acknowledged.

I somehow sputtered out, "Ye–ye–yes."

I felt the presence of this man stand more upright as He spoke, "If you knew who I was, you would not hesitate to say it."

Well, that prompted me to take my hand off my eyes and gradually look His way. As my eyes rose from the ground, there stood a man who I recognized without even seeing Him clearly in the distance, Someone my heart had already known was coming my way — and was now before me!

I saw the silhouette of a man with shoulder length hair that seemed to have a life of its own, moving to an unseen wind, but dancing like light rays off the sun. He had on a full-length, billowing white robe that stretched down past His feet. His face — well I don't remember seeing His face. I was looking in the vicinity of His face, but to say I outright saw it I cannot do, because I don't recall it.

His hands were at His sides, as He waited for my response, which didn't take long, I can assure you. But something happened in my saying His Name that later surprised me.

I responded, "Y–y–you're Jesus."

I didn't say His Name in my native English language though; I said it in the Spanish or former Yugoslavian version pronounced HAY-soos or teHAY-soos. Maybe I said it this way because of the manner in which people abuse His Name in conversation or overly use it in other forms, such as cursing. Whatever the reason, it felt not fully right to me to just simply say Jesus. I'm sure people tend to swear in other languages where Jesus' name is involved, but at least I don't hear it. Either way, Jesus didn't seem to mind; He knew what I meant.

He responded softly and with authority, "Yes, I am."

He then gracefully rose into the air, filling His garment with soft wind. Light then seemed to suddenly radiate around Him, making His form outlined even more so. Pure white light seemed to come from everywhere, making His face beam like a sun but still darkened against the brighter light behind Him. I believe it was this shadowing of His face and brightness around it at the same time that made it difficult to recall what His face might have looked like.

The light didn't hurt my eyes; it was almost nurturing, if anything. But I know that if I saw a light that intense now in everyday life, I would have to look away.

From the start of this encounter, something else was in the air, aside from the immediate recognition I felt. This "something" grew with more intensity when the light began to beam from this sun of the Son of God — Love!

If love could have a thickness or texture to show its wealth, brawn, or value at the market, this would have been the blue ribbon champion at the state fair! This man was 'Love'. The air around Him flooded with Love to buoyancy, and I was giddy with Love trickles from the inside out!

This Love level was in the air as He approached me, so it was there before I ever spoke to Him. So when He rose into the air and the light came forth, all of this Love just shot up into ridiculous levels that would be dizzying for me to even try to reenact!

I keep trying to think of more ways to describe what it all felt like, and even now while I'm writing this my heart races with desire to help me come up with the right words.

So let me have at it a bit here. I'll try to throw all of these emotions together to give a clearer picture of what I mean: It was a burning, spurning, churning, spiraling, lifting, walk-with-a-crick-in-your-back-only-to-have-it-straightened-out, cramp in your stomach smoothed out with pink liquid, winning your first race after an injury, triumphant with positive thinking over a wrong-doing, justice for the poor, getting an unexpected check in the mail for bills you thought would go unpaid, soul searching for the once thought heartless, bringing home a new puppy, joy at home with friends for the holidays, baby's first steps, seeing the light at the end of the tunnel, and being greeted by past friends, or to arrive home safely after a long drive in Wisconsin's winter weather!

Even still these words fall short in description.

So there I was, being met with G-force Love waves coming at me, with Jesus lit up and hovering now about three feet off the ground. His rise was gentle, as He began to speak about His life and what He aimed to do while He was upon the Earth.

I don't know if my mind was so in awe, if I wasn't able to fully pay attention, or that I wasn't meant to recall all of the details of what He said, because I didn't. It was as if He was "floating" His intentions to me, more than me actually hearing His Words about His life mission and accomplishments. Yet, I did hear His Voice, strong and whispered.

Essentially, it was as if flashes of His feelings overcame me, as scenes from a time long past went by my mind's eye with His Words guiding me. I was very much aware of who was in front of me talking, and how unbelievable all of this was. Yet, oddly enough, I started to drift off into my own thoughts, as Jesus continued to fill me with large amounts of His life intentions and information concerning those times. I looked around the sides of Him and thought how strange it was that He, indeed, was as many artists had depicted Him, with the long hair and flowing robe.

Many folks seem to focus on whether Jesus was white, brown, or black, and to tell you the truth, I didn't pay much mind to that. But if I think on it now, initially, I did mistake Him for Quincy, who is African-American. When He came closer, I honestly don't remember Him being very dark, but He was a bit more tan than what I've seen Him depicted as. But to say for certain what color He is, who really cares? All I'm truly concerned about is that He did and does exist. To get into odd little details at times just distracts from the reality of Him, I feel.

As I continued to look around Jesus, I then put my attention toward the ground. It seemed that the ground was awfully close to me, and I couldn't determine why that was for a moment, until I noticed, *I'm on my knees!* I exclaimed in my head. *I don't even remember going on my knees!*

I was astonished at my position, but I indeed felt conscious and aware of everything else going on. So much so that I could hardly believe and interpret all that was happening to me at the moment, and yet I did with ease. What a strange thing to say, but the more bewilderment I had, the calmer and more content I became.

Almost as if Jesus knew I wasn't paying attention as I should have, He paused as He was speaking to me. I felt a little rude, kind of like the kid passing notes in class only for the teacher to have to stop the lesson to see what was so important for me not to be paying attention. However, I didn't feel like His pause was scolding. It just seemed that He realized I was still a bit baffled and that I was taking the time to take it all in before I could pay attention fully.

So He stopped mid-sentence, and I looked up from the ground, knowing I had been getting off course and was needing to refocus on what He was saying. But instead of waiting to see if He was going to speak some more, I felt the need to ask Him humbly — with a stutter, "W–well, wh–what do you want me to do?"

After listening and taking in part of His lessons and actions from His days upon the Earth, it felt like a logical question to ask at the time. It was obvious that my God-given freewill was still intact, so my curious soul reacted as I would as my usual self when met with a situation requiring direction. I felt that Jesus listened to my question with complete patience and understanding.

Then the scene seemed to switch. He was now to the left of where I once was, and I seemed to be in a house of some kind. It felt like my parent's home still, yet it didn't look anything like it. The walls were mostly bare, and the color white seemed to be the main theme in this vast room that felt very comfortable, much like a family room would feel.

I was also standing upright now and facing Him where He now stood, about five feet from me. He then began to speak more directly, slowly, and compassionately, "First, you need to show us some things," He said.

Us? I wondered. He was the only one there whom I could see, so I could only imagine what He meant. But, then again, I somehow knew what He meant. It was as if He wanted to see if I'd stick things out for the long haul and dedicate myself to His efforts and perhaps His Father's.

"You need to finish your book. Do not be discouraged by what others say. Know that I will be there and give you the words . . ." He continued with more which I can not recall.

He then went on to tell of other things that I knew I was not *meant* to recall right away, but only when the time came for it to be needed. As He spoke these last instructions, I felt like I was looking through a pane of glass where I could see His lips moving but could not hear it with my ears anymore, only my heart. I felt this part of our discussion to be, by far, briefer than His life story which He had shared just before this.

Then the pane of glass was removed, and He paused for a few moments with what felt like a smile of satisfaction emitting from Him toward me. I somehow knew after this gesture that He had to go now and that it was going to be a sudden departure. I thought to myself, *How can I get more information to help me understand what I am supposed to do?* The first thing I could think of was an odd question, to say the least.

So there I was. I had Jesus before me, and He started to fade away into one of the white walls in this large room. He had nearly dissipated into the wall when I reached out to touch the spot He was disappearing into, and I asked, "Jesus, what's my real name?"

I then heard Him laugh lightly and say gently, "I love you very much, Ileyah!" (pronounced: iLEE-YAH)

I knew this experience was a grand one, but even so, whenever I had encounters of any otherworldly kind, I would forget details. Well, with this revelation holding so much weight and being given this name from Jesus, I was determined to remember that name.

I slowly slid my hand down as I pulled away from the wall, and all sight of Him was gone. I tipped my head forward and began repeating over and over in my mind this name, so I wouldn't dare forget. I knew this experience was about to end and wanted to hold onto it with all my heart and all my memories.

The scene began to fade away as if it were whitening out into nothingness. I then gently returned to my conscious body. I didn't want to move right away because His Love was still tingling in me, and I didn't want to let that floating feeling go. As I lay there, I could feel myself smiling while tears of joy streamed down my face.

I had seen Jesus, there was no doubt, and I sure didn't cry much for anything back then. When I actually did cry it was usually because of some act of kindness someone showed another. Whenever unconditional love was shown, it touched me more than acts of hate or pain. It hurt to see pain caused, or to feel it myself, but I didn't feel it nearly as much when love was being dispersed. (Conclusion: I guess love is a stronger emotion than hate after all.)

So there I lay, still basking in the love and now opening my eyes. I thought it would be a good idea to call for my roommate to share the extraordinary news, when suddenly it seemed almost like a dark curtain cut through my light and emotions. Dread overcame me as I realized that my ability to move was being robbed from me. I suddenly felt drugged, and my eyes quickly closed as I was abducted from this life and into a strange nightmare . . .

5

DARKNESS ARRIVES

"Where am I?"

Well, this started off all too familiar. I looked around my surroundings in this place that physically reminded me of another place but was all wrong. Darkness had grabbed and taken me here; I could feel it all around me. In this place there was anger, there was hate, and, most sickening of all, there was this putrid sense of rage pointed in my direction.

Somehow, in some way, I had been taken on yet another trip into the unknown. I looked more closely. This was a rendition of my parents' kitchen, looking out toward the family room. It was a lot larger, and crucial things were missing that would give it that comfy feeling or a three-dimensional "feel" to it. It was as if someone took a copy of my memory and pasted it in front of me with blue-screen movie technology.

As I gazed around, suddenly someone or something came up behind me and leaned over my left shoulder. I could feel the coldness in this thing's presence and stood steadfast, looking forward and wondering how shabby of a job this rendition of my parents' home was. Hey, I'm an artist (Drawing/writing comic strips and creating comical ceramic creatures are hobbies of mine.), and if things are not esthetically pleasing, I take note of it, vision or not.

I then turned my attention slightly toward this entity to see that it had taken on the form of a family member. But it wore the face of this person loosely, like an ill-fitting mask. There was no soul behind the face, easily noted since its eyes were blackened, making it quite disturbing to even look at, let alone having it stand so close to me. It began to speak to me in a lisp with snake-like pronunciations, dragging out every comment.

"Are you s–s–sure about what you s–s–saw?" It asked.

I looked at it, confused, wondering what it was asking about.

"Are you s–s–sure it wasn't Quincy you s–s–saw?"

My confusion turned to distaste, as I realized now what this thing was trying to get at, but I didn't say a word. Then it drew my attention to look where it was pointing when it said, "Look there now; there's Quincy! Was it him you s–s–saw?"

I looked straight ahead, and, sure enough, there appeared an image that looked very much like Quincy. It began to walk across the room at an angle, which made it come slightly closer to where I stood. I still said nothing and wondered what was going on and why.

Then the thing spoke up again, "There goes another Quincy! Are you s–s–sure it wasn't him you s–s–saw?"

Another image of Quincy appeared out of nowhere, strolled the length of the room, and came to a dead stop as if he'd reached the end of his rope as the other had.

"There goes another one, and another one, and another! Are you s–s–sure of what you s–s–saw!?"

It now demanded of me to declare where I stood, so I did just that, but with confusion and caution when I responded to it, "I don't know who you are or what you are trying to do. But I know who I saw and it was Je–"

I started to say His Name, when this thing almost lunged to put its hand over my mouth, but I knew it couldn't touch me. So, instead, it spoke up even louder to point out yet another Quincy. Then the thing slouched forward in disgust and backed away from me. I looked forward to see why it had moved away from me. I stood frozen, as all of the Quincys turned only their heads toward me — and some turned their heads unnaturally further than they should have been allowed.

I then heard a harsh sound that was like a thousand windows crashing and turned around to see yet another strange creature running toward me with an odd-looking dagger. I knew the Quincys now behind me were also charging my way — and they wanted my blood!

My mind quickly cried out for help from God. The creature reached me and pulled his dagger back high over his head to stab me, when I suddenly felt yanked out of the situation and back into my body!

I could barely move for the first few moments once I arrived back. I felt drained from the darkness and terror of the experience I'd just had, but I soon managed to reach above my head and wildly pound on my bedroom wall to get my roommate's attention.

My roommate rushed into the room and asked, "What's the matter?"

Between deep breaths and trembling lips, I began to tell her what had happened. I had just had one of the most tremendous experiences in my life, and darkness had tried to cover it up. But I wouldn't let it, I was still overwhelmed by my visitation from Jesus, and it was the first thing out of my mouth. I initially still hadn't the strength to fully sit up in my bed, so I laid there as I began to relay my story. The more I spoke of Jesus, the more strength I gathered, until I was able to sit upright at the edge of my bed with full energy and charisma. I spoke in great detail of my encounter with Him, and then finally lent some discussion about the darkness that came to get me afterward.

My roommate, being a pretty spiritual person herself, was more than understanding about the impact of what had just happened to me.

She left the room shortly thereafter, and I remained on my bed, trying to interpret my unexpected trip.

I had just seen Jesus. But why?

I didn't feel worthy, not by a long shot. Then to also be paid another type of visit by something dark, without definition? I wondered why it was so important to those dark creatures to convince me that nothing had taken place with Jesus. Would it really have made a difference if simple little words of confusion had left my lips?

If I had said something like, "Maybe I was mistaken, but I thought it was Him," would that have been room enough for them to feed my doubts?

"If you give an inch, they'll take a mile." That's a saying I have heard all my life from my parents. I think that's very much the same philosophy I've learned to take in dealing with things that are dark now, too. Obviously, there was some weight to my words that this creature tried so hard to get some out of me. We *are* a society of beings who expresses ourselves verbally, since we haven't learned the Jedi Masters (of Star Wars fame) method of telepathy or power of suggestion, just yet. So we do tend to rely on the fact that we say what we mean, and mean what we say.

Many people say rotten things and say, "Well, yeah, I said it, but you know I didn't mean it." Well, if I'm reading this right, words do indeed take on intention whether you have a whole lot of feeling behind them or not. Yipes! That's such a scary thought when I think about that, too.

All of the negative things I have ever said that I knew I didn't mean (but worked just fine for me at the moment) carry weight! Now I'm beginning to wonder what kind of soul damage I might have done, or if I created some force of intention somewhere, somehow.

What if I'd said to that dark creature, "Gee, I'm not certain what I saw," instead? I bet any amount of money that I would be a consciously confused individual if any of that vision stuff happened or not. Heck, I might not have even made it out of that dark encounter, for all I know. Something did rescue me from that dagger-swinging scoundrel, and it wasn't because I cooperated with them.

To meet Jesus was more than a treat to come my way, with His message and meaning. He had something to say, to show me. But those dark savages; what was their true purpose, and why did they make such an obvious effort?

Jesus would know I would take His Presence to heart, so was the other presence there to rip it from me? Did they want me to feel their rage against His Presence? Or did they simply want to quiet me from telling anyone by threatening me and planting some doubting thoughts in my head?

There was so much to ponder, but I promised myself that I wouldn't take up too much of my energy and time to look at the fumblings of this crazy clan of Shadows or demons. But it sure was funny how they didn't seem to take too kindly that I wouldn't buy into their little "Quincy game".

I don't see how my simple words would or could have changed my heart about the situation in the first place, but it obviously seemed to make a difference to them that I stood my ground. If even simple words can take on shape and effort in the spiritual world, it makes more sense why they wanted to hear some confession of doubt.

It also makes sense why they didn't want to hear one simple name — Jesus. It felt like that creature wanted to rip my vocal chords out to stop me from speaking His Name. I am sure that it would have caused a burning sensation in their ears and would have sent them running in the opposite direction instead of at me. All I know is that when they came running, I felt like I threw my heart to God for help without words, just intentions. It seems that is all it took to get His attention, because I sure didn't feel that dagger that was wielded my way.

Wow, they were so quick to respond to Jesus coming my way, just so very fast. They really wanted to nip it before it got spread that Jesus was near and helping people. How close those dark things were; how desperate they were; it all just blows my mind still.

Well, that's just too bad. I guess I am now their worst nightmare come true, because I have this little problem in keeping my mouth shut on important things that need to be said.

Jesus just so happens to be one of those important things.

6

OPENING UP AND SAYING "BLAH"

~Tidbit: Don't you sometimes wish that the author of the book you are reading would just keep flowing with the good stuff and not always take the time to express what she feels about everything? You don't? Well, then you won't mind my babbling on in this chapter about how I interpreted this encounter with round and round analogies. For those of you who are like me, who could do without this personal angle sometimes, don't worry — it gets more interesting after this.~

I felt that after having dealt with so many strange things all my life, I was prepared to meet and deal with just about anything. Adding up my odd experiences as something no one could relate to was the norm for me, so it was easier for me to bite my tongue on a lot of things. But, holy moly, meeting Jesus was nothing to keep tightlipped about, and I surely couldn't help myself but had to share this incident.

I still realized that this all fell into the "No one can relate" category. However, most people seem to acknowledge that there is a God, and many even believe that His Son came here for a mission to save our souls. So, by having some people out there with some sense of Jesus made it much easier for me to share this particular experience with others.

Believe me when I say it was more therapeutic for me to tell what happened in the beginning than my trying to spread any "message" initially. I had hoped some of that good message stuff spilled in there, of course, but I was just bursting at the seams to tell anyone who cared to chat on the God and Jesus topic.

First things first; I didn't want to forget what meeting Jesus felt like from the inside out. I wanted to be sure, so, when I actually started speaking to others, I wouldn't lose any of the luster where the experience could grow dull.

As strange as it might sound, tremendous experiences that are outside of this so-called reality can be hard to keep a grip on. It's like once you are back here in the "now", the "then" seems like a distant dream, seemingly too incredible to have actually happened.

So, I held on tight to what everything felt like, and I wasn't going to let any influences flaw the experience. However, I knew that I would be up against some unique obstacles with my publicly known past of researching paranormal topics. My heart knew the truth of my Jesus experiences , and *I* knew the truth of my experiences, but how would all this appear to the rest of the world?

In my last book, *The Secret War*, I truly spoke of spiritual agendas, which involved what many people report as alien beings. I didn't find much difference between the stories of alien abductions, where people are being tortured by alien creatures, and the Biblical references of demons doing the same. Stories of positive forces of the so-called alien realm also didn't seem to be much different from stories of angels coming here to fight the more negative or demonic-like beings.

Yet, I know when people hear the term "alien" that there's this automatic image that pops into people's heads of those involved in the topic. There's no rationalizing about the millions of people in the world who don't know each other, yet they still report the same types of beings doing the same types of things to people. There's

45

also no thinking about the ridicule a person might have to go up against in society for just coming forth with a story so seemingly farfetched. There's not even the thought that there might be a closet family member, friend, or stranger who has had an experience outside of societal norms. Nope, there's none of this.

There only exists the thought that some uneducated, crazy-talking, devil-worshipping, cult-member fool is talking about there being aliens in our midst. This is the part where I come into the world and share that I'm pretty much known for being the "Alien Advice" giver on all sorts of mysterious topics — Oh! Uh... I happen to have seen Jesus, too.

Trust me; it's dawned on me that I was going to be looked at as some kind of weirdo trying to blend Jesus with UFOs and maybe make a new religion out of it all, or something, like, "Oh, great! She's into UFOs, and now she sees Jesus, too! Boy, do we have a live one here! This ought to be a darned interesting cult to watch for on the news. I wonder when the poisonous drinks will be dispensed and sipped."

What a harsh reality I was about to step into — and I knew it. People were going to judge me left and right and think I was looking for glory and perhaps even some "Hallelujahs!" My, my, even the UFO community might think of me as going AWOL, treading into territory where these things should not be mixed.

Wowzers! What a lot to think about if I planned on coming forward with my Jesus encounter. I did think about it — for about two seconds before I came back with, "Oh well!"

Jesus dropped a bomb my way for a reason. If He figured I could handle it, then who was I to say He was wrong?

So all that pondering was pretty much a no-brainer. I mean, *come on*; Jesus walks up to you and asks you to do something and you are going to be *shy* about it? I think not, which equals "no-brainer".

So, yeah, I meant to chat on the topic of Jesus a bit after His visit, but with discretion, so as not to freak out anyone too badly. I was still known for being into the paranormal arena, and, so, with most people I still had to speak about Jesus with caution.

I must admit, too, that I have a past where I played upon the teasing and thoughts that, "If you are into the paranormal, then you are into the devil-worshipping" gig. With strangers, I stood firmly with the facts that I wasn't into the devil/alien-worshipping thing. But my friends would toy with me about that same concept of devils and aliens, and I'd play along and say things like, "I'll probably catch on fire if I set a foot in a church."

For me, at that time, I found organized religion to be unnecessary for soul advancement and overrated to have to belong to one. So my comments did reflect my distaste for attending church. As far as my catching fire, because of my paranormal affiliation, that was just me and my odd sense of humor talking.

I've since learned some of my friends actually took me seriously about this kind of joking and interpreted it as my having a lack of faith in God. I can see how that might be thought of if the people I was speaking to hadn't known me better. But I thought those people did, so who knows why my faith seemed to wane to them.

Either way, when I went to some of my friends to relate what I had experienced in seeing Jesus, they seemed to recognize a change in me. One of my friends even commented that something incredible must have happened for me to talk about Jesus, of all people, because I didn't go to church! I don't see the relation between the ability to see Jesus that you must attend church, but that's what she told me.

But that was okay if a person believed that you had to be in church for something miraculous to happen. What did it hurt for me to hear?

Having perspectives like that abounding still didn't keep my mouth shut or my miracle any less of a reality. Even at work, I didn't care if I got strange looks about what I was relaying. I didn't just burst out with it either; I had some reserve.

Who am I kidding? I still looked for ways to bring it up, for my own sake as well as others. For instance, I recall how I spoke to one of my co-workers who had several children:

I asked, "Do your kids go to church?"

My co-worker responded that they did, and I said, "Good, keep them going, because Jesus is For Real, and He's coming back." Then I just kept toiling with my regular tasks.

Smooth! Drop a bomb and keep them wondering where the heck that came from. I was such an anxious amateur.

My co-worker looked at me and wondered why I would say such a thing, since it was a bit out of character for me to speak of something religious to her. I then told her what I had seen, but I left out the part of the dark creatures that came afterward. However, no matter who I spoke to or how I came to relate the story, I was always sure to finish it off and say, "Jesus is no joke!"

After saying this, it was almost as if nothing else needed to be said.

I'm generally known for not keeping a straight face. I'm always chuckling or cracking jokes and having a good time. Meeting Jesus was not a joking matter, and I never presented it to anyone as such. But when I went to speak on how all of His emotions and His Presence hit me personally, it was back to the same silly Heidi. Saying Jesus was not a joke kind of summed up how I really felt, and yet it let a part of my personality make its presence known, too.

It wasn't easy, trying to fully relate how it all felt to be in the presence of such a being as Jesus. It's especially hard when you are a goofball, yet you really want people to understand what you mean. So I learned to relate my Jesus encounter pretty much as if I were talking to a friend, which is the way I normally speak to anyone. I'd hoped it would let people know that I didn't have to change who I was just to relate something that even I considered most holy.

So, a typical conversation about my encounter with Jesus might start with something like, "I was like, 'Holy crap, I can't believe this is happening!' Yappity, yap, yap . . ."

Yet, when the story went to talking on Jesus, Himself, and how He felt to me and what He said, it was like I couldn't help but flow more seriousness into the conversation, especially when I started talking about how I recognized Him. I couldn't help but say exactly how it felt. It was the one part of the story that seemed essential to me, because people always raised the question about how I knew who this man was. I tell people, "I could have been blind and known who it was in front of me! Every cell in my body seemed to scream His Name!"

That was all surely the truth.

It's hard to describe being able to feel all of your cells work in unison to tell you something. I didn't know my cells had anything on their mind other than keeping me functioning properly to live, but they spoke, all right. They recognized and they acknowledged the Son of God!

There's no other way to put it or share it with other people, than how it's been said for so long: He is indeed the Creator's Son, our Savior, and our Messiah. I don't know how or why and I'm not one for getting into senseless details; the man just was and is, if you know what I mean.

Things started to change for me quite drastically after my encounter with Jesus. Not only did He give me a new mystery to ponder, but He also moved me to look at all of my odd and strange experiences in a whole different light. Talking or relating about mysterious topics, as I had done before, had gone to a level way beyond anything I thought I could reach.

When I met Jesus, He had asked me to finish my book, of all things. Well, the book I was touching up here and there at the time was my first book, *The Secret War: The Heavens Speak Of The Battle*. This book, as I've mentioned, entailed the conflict between positive and negative beings visiting Earth and what they were up to with these visits. So, by Jesus mentioning this book, it acknowledged to me that there was indeed a problem between the negative and positive forces or beings — however people want to define them.

~Tidbit: It's just too bad that people can get caught up in definitions while truths might pass them by. My fingers are crossed that people will be able to adjust if reality doesn't play out the way some of them expect it to, where only winged deities and horned beasts will fight in this conflict, in this battle between good and evil. Having the ability to flush one's pride down the toilet if they are wrong in their spiritual assumptions, I'm finding, is a much-needed skill to develop. Strength of character, perky wit, and a firm grip with quick wrist action for flushing is a must, if I may pass on some of the newly acquired traits which I've had to learn while awakening into my new spiritual reality.

~Tiny Tidbit: Jesus promised me He would give me the words to help get points across to people, but don't take the above note as a direct quote from Him. ☺

For me, it was like getting a registered letter from Jesus that let me know that I was on the right track with the topic I wrote on.

I also had some fun writing that book, where I once again took a serious topic, which I didn't try to make light of, and spoke of it more casually than most. It's a habit of mine, I suppose, and I don't intend to break it. I like to think that having a sense of humor makes some of this stuff just a little easier to take in.

Jesus, Himself, didn't seem to be so stressed out that He couldn't let a part of His soul echo, even. The light laughter that Jesus sent my way just before He vanished told me a lot about Him, that He really had quite a sense of humor! His laugh was sincere and hearty. Although it was as light as the music from a flute, it really bellowed from His soul.

But there was something more than just that laugh. There was something that made me feel as if He was a friend — and I mean the best friend I could ever have, one who might even give you light punches as you joke together.

What a strange thing to say, but then to know that He wouldn't take offense at being referred to as a friend is even more awesome! That feeling of being fun, in the light of being good, just seems to go together when talking about Jesus. So, I've done my best to bring some of that sunshine in when I speak about Him, because it's just so fitting for Him.

The experience with Jesus was a grand one, but I couldn't fool myself into realizing that it didn't happen without a consequence. Darkness followed up my experience with a reminder that they were never far behind.

I didn't know how to immediately share this dark experience with others only if it was to share a warning. I was a newbie at speaking to anyone on such a topic, and questions on doing it the right way filled my mind all of the time.

The odd thing is, even with all of the questions that came forward in me, I felt so content with answers after meeting Him. I still had this first book of mine in my lap that had been technically done, yet I still did some editing here and there until it actually got published. Not to mention that I had to fully rewrite the chapter that spoke of visions of Jesus as being misinterpretations of angels.

After that book's first publication in October of 2001, I got some interesting feedback. I received a couple of letters from readers asking about my Jesus encounter that I mentioned in the book. I had to put it in there, of course.

One guy asked me where that came from, as if he could tell that this sudden Jesus encounter was not part of the original frame and angle of the chapter. I complimented him on being so observant and for taking the time to write. I then told him that the encounter was as much a shock for me as it was for him to see it in there, but I wasn't about to leave it out.

With that, I could tell that my priorities were starting to change. The whole lot of paranormal topics that I looked into didn't fully answer all of what was really important. Even as my first book developed, I saw it change into a more spiritual entity, taking on its own life, inside and outside of me. It was the spiritual message that I wrote about that inspired me to write it to begin with. Speaking out about positive and negative agendas was moving for me, and all, but when it came to Jesus, there was just no comparison.

After that book's publication, I started to get booked for radio interviews and speaking engagements. I had (and still have) a terrible case of stage fright, and I flat out dreaded the thought of having to speak to more than one person at a time on anything contained in my book, or otherwise. Of course, I wanted to let people hear what was in the book or what I felt was important to know about it, but it's hard when you are battling yourself to get anything done.

I continued to be booked to the point where I was successful in filling my whole year for events across the country, much to my surprise! However, each time I got another gig, I asked myself, *What am I doing?* But I knew I had to do this because it was too important to let it go. Jesus had asked me to finish this book.

Yes, it was Jesus who kept rolling around in my head each time I thought about not wanting to do any of these public speaking engagements. My anxiety was tremendous each and every time I thought about having to speak anywhere. Even months in advance, my stomach would sink into a slump at the thought of lecturing again. Then I would think about what Jesus had told me, how He had promised to give me the words to speak with, and how He had told me not to worry about what others said.

So, when time came where I would be just about to walk up to the lectern or if I was sitting home waiting to do a radio interview, I started a routine. I would look up briefly toward the ceiling and say, "Jesus, you promised you would give me the words, and I'm holding you to it!"

Well, I wasn't lying! Each time I say that with my eyes turned up toward the heavens, I imagine Him laughing, nodding His head to go on, and that He'll be there.

So far, so good, He hasn't failed me yet. It doesn't mean that my knees don't jitter or my palms don't sweat before going out on stage (although I wish they would stop). I feel confident in Him and His Word, but it's the "me" part acting up that I have a hard time controlling.

Only through Him have I been able to get through my days to accomplish what I have in my writings and talks. Little did people know that this supposed UFO lady didn't get her information out on her own. There is no way I would have been able to continue or even begin to do what I have done had I not had His Shoulder to lean on and outright know that I could. I cannot begin to express how hard it was to stick to a subject so seemingly farfetched, where it even halted my studied career in being an occupational therapist, much to everyone's disapproval. It was a lonely, financially broken, unfamiliar, stay indoors to write, rusty car driving, chosen path. It was not easy in any capacity, and, even now, while I'm writing this book, most of these same issues still come my way. But I was always fortunate, because I was lucky enough to know that Jesus was literally on my side.

Why people choose not to understand why a person feels passionate about something, when they personally do not, baffles me. Since my encounter, I have found contentment in so many ways that I wish others could feel and find. After meeting Jesus, I have a passion so strong that I find it difficult to judge anyone for being passionate about what they believe to be true, no matter how odd it might all sound, even to me — the supposed Queen of the Strange.

All of us have opinions about what others might believe. Now I can look past the superficial outside of what might seem strange to me in someone's beliefs and see the heart of the person.

If a person thinks Elvis is hiding out and not dead, fine! If a person thinks the Egyptians put meaning into every inch of the pyramids for descendents to decipher centuries later, great! If a person thinks there's no life on other planets and has dedicated their life to prove it, awesome! If a person believes Jesus was no greater than the next person, uh, okay — although they would be wrong!

Oops, there I go judging again. Here I thought I had that under wraps. I guess it's truly hard for anyone to be fully non-judgmental.

Yet, I can understand the confusion regarding Jesus and what He's all about now, so I really shouldn't judge.

Back to this thing about a person's passion: It's hard to point out something in someone's heart and tell them that it's wrong. It doesn't hurt me to know what another person vibes with, but, for some reason, I have learned that insecure people will try to throw their beliefs your way. If you feel secure about where you are coming from, then there's patience if there's something you feel needs to be said.

If an atheist is screaming how there's no God and how all are being misled, hear them out and see where they are coming from. It doesn't change who you are at all to hear it, and you might get the chance to share where you are coming from and be listened to with just as much respect as you showed that atheist person. If they don't, then they are not secure enough to even hear another's perspective, and they need to be left alone.

With the contentment that came to me through my Jesus encounter, I learned there was a way to talk to people with understanding. I didn't feel a need to tell people to convert to the laws of God or throw Biblical quotes at people, besides, I hardly knew any. I would just talk about me and my belief so I didn't banter it like it was gospel, but I shared a part of me and what I felt in seeing Him in all of my silly human words. I was just "me" and no airy words, no raising of my voice to ensure that others were enthralled by my presence, or anything.

Being me was the only way I knew how to speak about Jesus or any other topic. I wasn't out to convince anyone about odd things; I was content in knowing what I did and what I'd experienced.

I also understood that the people I spoke to most likely had no experience to fully relate to what I was talking about.

I was the lucky one who got to be content, secure, and even patient all at once by seeing Jesus. Sure, I was anxious to share the story of seeing Him and feeling His Love. If I could even get an ounce of that Love out of me to show to another, I would. Jesus brought me Love and truly let me see how such a small word could mean so much. I had my ache filled by Him, and I was, and am, more than happy to put it use.

I wonder if Jesus is happy that He's having to own up to the promise He made, giving me the words that I need. I wonder if He ever gets writer's block, too, because I haven't had any problems on this end in what needs to be said — yet.

Keep giving the words, Jesus, and I'll keep writing them.

CHAPTER

7

HERE HE COMES AGAIN

My whole angle, and, seemingly, my whole goal in life was starting to change, and I doubt if I was fully aware just how much. There would come a time when I knew I would speak more formally about my experience with Jesus. For the moment, however, that time wasn't upon me.

Ready or not, there was soon more to come my way. I never wanted to appear as if I were anything more than a fellow pew sitter. Jesus must have sat in the pew next to me, because He had a few more things that He wanted to share.

The new millennium was just around the corner; lots of celebration and despair loomed in the air at the same time. The party of all parties was going to be thrown for this newly numbered year, which was a long time coming. To many people, this time also spelled fear that the infamous Y2K bug was near (Wow! — That rhymed.), the almighty bug that never was. This glitch was to put the world on hold due to our silly judgment and reliance on computers that weren't designed to change from the 1900s into 2000s.

Perhaps some of the people who programmed this error didn't think we would make it this far to see the new millennium, who knows? At least my cheap VCR, which was nine years old, got the picture and was able to change over. Yipes! To think that I would have to go out and buy another one just horrified me (sarcasm at its sweetest).

There was a great number of people I met then who spoke of conspiracy theories and other talk of our world changing in ways unimaginable due to the Y2K bug, so I knew of a great many horrid possibilities.

I was very much a social bug who liked to go out and dance, but I was never into the club scene, where often drugs and drinking seemed to overwhelm the crowds I'd see out and around those days. However, I did receive quite a few invitations to various parties at clubs, at houses, and even at large vacant warehouses where parties were being organized just for the occasion of the new year and the millennium.

It would strike me in waves as to how I would celebrate the new millennium. I thought how this truly was going to be the celebration of a lifetime. But then I'd think on how smoky and crowded the nightclubs would be, as usual. I also started hearing of millenium/Y2K pranks planned by some people who were in charge of warehouse parties. One person even told me how they were going to turn the electricity off at midnight, as if to show the Y2K bug had appeared in the matrix.

I imagined the hundreds of people drunkenly trampling each other, trying to clear out of the joint in a wild panic. People I knew, and even strangers, would share their thoughts of what wild thing they wanted to be doing when the clock struck midnight. It started to feel weird for me to think that this singly measured second passing by was going to make all the difference on how life would play out for me into the next millennium.

I began to see no point in the rush to gyrate my body to the rhythm of some music I wished the DJ would change to something recognizable, just to be able to say I had brought in the new millennium doing that. So I called up my folks and planned to have a more

57

meaningful event, a night of laughs, food, playing cards, and watching New York's Times Square do the usual Dick Clark ensemble.

So, by December 30, I was at peace about my millennium plans and couldn't think of anything more meaningful and relaxing than bringing it in with my folks and one of my good friends.

I turned into bed around my usual midnight bedtime and nestled in the blankets, my armor against the chilly air that persisted outside, which unfortunately intruded into my room through an old window. Once I fought through the onslaught of the chill upon my sheets and bed and heated things up through uncontrollable jitters which my body dished out, I started to drift off to sleep.

I don't know how long I slept before something curious woke me up. Through my closed eyelids, I could see something new was in the room. I then opened my eyes to see that there was an intense light in my room, as white as I've ever seen. The room seemed warm, as if daylight sunshine had brought summer into my room. I was lying with my back flat against the bed, and I pushed up with my elbows to prop myself up to get a better view of where this light was coming from. I looked directly toward the source of the light, which was peering at the foot of my bed.

My bed fit perfectly into one corner of this extremely small bedroom where the foot and head of the bed touched the wall on both ends and one full side of the bed was against another wall. This room almost looked as if it had been constructed around my bed to allow room only for that full-sized mattress and my desk. So to think of there being a light source coming from the foot of the bed was bewildering. I knew that it could be no normal source since normally there was nothing but a wall there.

I looked down to where my feet made a rising lump in the blankets and saw what looked like a ray of sunlight, just as it might look when it streams through fluffy white clouds with noticeable layers of light. The light was coming about midway out of the wall and hitting my covered feet directly. I partially moved the thicker top layer of my blankets to the side to get a better look at what I was seeing. In utter amazement, I started to see parts of this light break into small sparkles that swirled and swooped and started moving up my legs.

Having known what the presence of Jesus already felt like and my body cells having so much to say, once again, I immediately said in my mind, *It's Him again!*

Love poured into me as the light sparkles moved up toward my stomach. I remained propped up on my elbows in absolute awe.

I wondered why I couldn't directly see Him. Instead, I only felt His Presence, just as powerfully as I had before. Once the light reached my stomach, it began to swirl slowly, and the tail end of the light sparkles seemed to gather in this swirling mass.

When all of the sparkles gathered, something tremendous happened; Jesus' presence filled me with incredible euphoria. I felt that my soul would explode in sheer delight. Then, suddenly, as I lay there propped up and watching, I slipped right out of my body!

I felt as if I were resting on a netted hammock swinging in the wind, when, suddenly, a big gust of air blew me and my hammock upside down, and I found myself staring at the ground. It was just as smooth and much in the same motion as a hammock would swing, because, suddenly, I found myself swooped up and looking down at my body, as I hovered a few feet above it!

I was amazed at what had just happened and how swiftly I had been twirled to look down at my body from above. The euphoria dimmed slightly and changed to a more spiritual delight and excitement now that I was in spiritual form. I wasn't a bit disappointed by the lessening of the feeling, since now I was able to concentrate more on what was going on and why, as odd as that may seem. It was not like my senses got blocked from what was happening. There was an overwhelming emotion of love to the "nth degree", which made it harder to think of all the things I might generally think about when in His kind of Presence.

So, there I hovered, looking and wondering why Jesus wasn't speaking. He wasn't saying anything, but I could tell He was working on something with me.

As I continued to look on, I thought about what He might be doing to me, as I watched the swirling light pick up speed.

Then a tremendous thought popped into my mind, *Is He healing me!?*

I had been diagnosed as having ulcerative colitis for nearly ten years, which proved to be a huge pain when it came to anything entering my digestive system (on more levels than I care to count). Then I recalled (This is where the human "me" kicks in.) when a friend related a message to me from a spiritual being who said those like him didn't do healings so as not to create followers, which would distract from God. This was told to me in regard to my asking if my disease could be healed by one of these spiritual beings I've experienced at different times in my life.

So, when I questioned and wondered if Jesus was healing me, what this being had related to my friend popped into my head. Automatically, then, I thought I knew the answer, as I truly felt my disappointment resonate in my soul when I thought, *No, He wouldn't do that.* Meaning, Jesus wouldn't heal me, because if one positive being wouldn't, why would He?

Upon drawing this conclusion, while still out of my body, the light that was hitting my blanket covered feet ceased coming from the wall. The swirling mass that was in my stomach area continued for a few moments more, then stopped, and I watched as it was absorbed into my body. Just then, my upside-down hammock swung me back into my body with the same quickness that it had swung me up.

I quickly patted my stomach to see if I was truly back and to feel if I felt physically different. I looked around the room to see if His Presence was still near, but He was indeed gone. I could still feel His Presence all over my insides and in my heart, though. I somehow knew He had left something with me, but what it could be I was not fully aware.

I closed my eyes and said a silent prayer of thanks for His visit, asked questions about why He had come without a word, and wondered if there was something more I should know or had missed. I got no immediate response and wondered continuously about the meaning of His visit.

Following this encounter, I somehow felt different in my soul about my role in this life and that something truly needed to be said about His very real existence.

I shared what happened with my parents at our new millennium get together, and I got the, "That's interesting, dear," sort of response. Nothing offensive from my folks, just more like, "I'm sure it was real to you, but I can't relate, so I'll just smile, nod, and offer you something to drink to bring in the New Year."

I had just experienced Jesus for the second time, making me twice less likely to be understood by anyone, so, sure, why not toast the New Year? Nothing too toasty though, one reason being that I didn't like to drink much and the other being that I wanted my mind clear to continue pondering on why Jesus physically stopped by this time.

It took until October of 2002 for me to realize my grand mistake in interpreting Jesus' visit that evening. That was when I went back to my doctor for a complete check-up (full biopsies and so on) to see how my disease was doing. I continued to have symptoms of colitis: bloating, cramps, and beloved diarrhea — a great word to mention in a Jesus book, by the way. I had been diagnosed as having a mild case of colitis, but I didn't see how continuously burning a route to the bathroom could be considered "mild" for anyone trying to function in this life.

A few days later I got a call from my doctor with the results of my tests. He sounded a bit puzzled when he said, "I can't find the disease."

Now I was confused.

After several months, and literally up until April 18th, 2003, my doctor thought that it might just be a misdiagnosis — after twelve years of being considered a colitis sufferer! There is no cure for this autoimmune disorder (aside from removing the colon) where the body tends to attack itself and cause inflammation and ulcers in the large intestine, among other problems and increased cancer risk.

My doctor thought it might be a bacterium that caused my problems, but I had been tested for that with no results proving that to be the case. I was asked to try taking some friendly bacteria to bring some balance back to my system and see if it would help my situation.

Before I went out and purchased the bacteria, I didn't let reality sink into my head that perhaps I was healed — that Jesus had cured me a couple of years back.

Upon first hearing the news that they could not see my disease, I was stunned and disbelieving. I asked why I still had the symptoms of the disease and was met with silence. That's when I was offered the holistic approach of the bacteria pill.

I hung up the phone and drove to buy the good bacteria. As I drove, I thought of the time when Jesus came to me in a light and focused on my stomach area. But had He healed me?

I thought hard as I continued to drive. I wanted relief from my symptoms in any way possible after twelve years of havoc and headache. If anything would help, I was game for it.

I purchased the bacteria, got home, took a couple of pills, and sat down to think, *If He healed me, I would have noticed a difference in my health, wouldn't I?* The bacteria seemed to help me, but my realization of the possibility that Jesus had healed me started to seep into my mind even more. I knew that doctors had a tendency to try to explain things away which have no explanation.

Through direct biopsies and videos of these procedures shown to me by my doctor, he revealed that my disease had progressed from involving one part of the colon to the entire colon. Does that happen and were my test results typical of someone with this disease? I tried to get clearer answers but only seemed to get replies that I should just be happy that whatever it was is gone.

Had I been so naïve to think that when that spiritual being said that they didn't do healings that it included Jesus?

A few weeks later I got together with a group I run, where we discuss any topic that's out of the ordinary. By mere coincidence the subject of healings came up. There was a woman there who was clearly disabled and had come once before and wanted to know why certain people get ill while others did not. She had also tried to get healed by people who claimed to do healings and wanted to know if aliens could and would do that for her.

Others in the group were quick to point out something that most of us who have ever heard anything about Jesus' life already knew — He was a healer. It was also pointed out that He was only apt to heal those who had faith in God. So the woman who was seeking healing was told to direct her desire to be healed to the only One capable of doing it — Jesus!

I could have placed a dunce cap on my head and called it a day after hearing that! Instead, I found the courage to speak up and acknowledge that this is what I felt had happened to me.

"I think Jesus healed me."

Attention quickly turned my way, and I went on to explain something I felt then that I should have realized a long time ago about what had taken place that night. I had doubted what He was doing and His ability to do so, and that's when the light went out and absorbed into me. I didn't have faith about anything that was happening, only because I had listened to "me" and my silly logic.

What the spiritual being had said was true, he didn't say he could or would heal me, but Jesus was a totally separate entity with unending abilities. I simply wasn't accepting what my soul saw, but I was in the "know" of what Jesus could do. I just don't know how I could have kept it out of mind for so long.

Once I began to understand that it was Jesus who had put the fixings on me, I knew that I didn't need to carry on indefinitely with the friendly bacteria pill as my doctor had suggested. I had accepted in my mind what appeared to have taken place, and my body responded accordingly where my symptoms subsided, after I acknowledged Jesus' capabilities and intentions.

Just for the record: After finding there was a whole slew of good reasons to take friendly bacteria called acidophilus (the same that's in yogurt), I did take the pills every once in a while. Also, with my doctor's advice, I avoided certain over-the-counter pain relievers that could cause symptoms similar to mine. A couple of years after my healing realization and living symptom free of colitis, my digestive system began to react sensitively to changes in my diet after returning back to the U.S. from another country. So, I now resemble someone who may be called an Irritable Bowel Syndrome (IBS) sufferer, although not diagnosed nor is it a dire case. But to know for certain what was the cause of my original illness — was it all a misdiagnosis, or was it a coincidence in the timing that I realized what Jesus could do — I didn't know at the moment. This is not something I'm being evasive about. If I'm personally wrong in what I perceive as a healing, then so be it.

Either way, I learned a valuable lesson in all of this that can do nothing but help the next person. If we are in doubt or lack faith, then our reality plays out in the same manner, so then what could be miracles for you won't come to be a reality. It seems the physical body has such a grip on our emotions that it holds our thoughts in bondage, which creates a captive audience to our experiences and not always to what's behind them.

I also learned to set my thoughts and heart free when it came to Jesus, especially after this realization of His gift to me. He offers so much to us all so much of the time, but if we are not there to even acknowledge what He is offering, how can it be fully received? I now know that having Him only shadowing our lives to help and protect us is not enough, if we don't turn to take His hand in the journey in all that stands before us in this reality which only He and His Father fully understand.

8

FINDING MEANING

Healed or misdiagnosed, however people will interpret it, my faith went up a notch. Jesus had come once again!

I didn't feel all that worthy, of course, and I still don't, because I think we all feel guilty to some extent that we fall short of God or His Son making any special visits.

People often ask me, "Why you, Heidi? Why do you think He came to you?" In thinking about this question, I believe what we all should be asking ourselves is, "Why not me?"

I'm the first to say that I am no one special, but some people still have asked, "Why do you suppose you got the privilege of meeting Him?"

Yet again, I believe we all have the same access, but few realize it in their souls. Much like my doubting Jesus, who is right there practically saying, "Hello, Heidi, wake up!" I still doubted who He was by doubting what He was capable of and had been known for doing since the beginning of His time on Earth.

I know some of you might be wondering as you read this, *What was she thinking in doubting His healing abilities?* While I'm thinking, *What are those people thinking that they can't experience Him, too?* It goes both ways.

My flub in judgment seems hilarious, yet I was in the same situation, in that I never thought I would or could see Jesus.

I never thought of meeting Him as a goal. Heck, I didn't even think He was the main character in the Bible, but that God was. Jesus was cool and all, but why get to know Him any better? I thought about a lot of things in my life, aside from, "I bet I can experience that Jesus guy if I really rub my eyes hard and turn on a strobe light or something."

Now some psychology professor with all of his authority might say, "The mind is a limitless thing and can create any reality you wish for." Meaning, "If you read the words of this book, you will think that you can experience Jesus and He will appear, but it will have been your wishful thinking alone."

For those who choose to look to the research end of this sort of thing, I can offer an interesting tidbit of information which I came across: Michael Willesee, who has done award-winning research as a skeptical journalist on psychic ability, dowsing, and acupuncture, became convinced of the miracles of holy visions and other related phenomena through his investigations. He found what he claimed to be factual as well as scientific evidence which supported these seemingly tremendous claims. His work was featured in a special documentary program aired by Fox, and it was entitled *Signs from God: Science Tests Faith.*

Of course, his investigation soon became a target for other skeptics who were no doubt much like himself at one time. Yet, I'm one of those open-minded folks who likes to think that the intention of a skeptical journalist remains that way, unless convinced of something else. A good journalist is an honest and objective one. If he were to back down and drop his investigation because the findings didn't support his targeted hypothesis, I think his integrity could then be questioned. Putting the work forward and out there for the world to see and decide for themselves about what is represented works best.

For me, Willesee's findings revealed that quite a few folks have claimed to have visions of Jesus (among other holy visions).

Are all of these claims made by a bunch of wishful thinkers or concocters of coincidence? Or are some simply hoaxes?

Perhaps we all called each other and asked how our Jesus encounter should be portrayed. Especially how we should present it to our friends and family to be sure we can get their eyes to roll and their bellies to rumble with laughter in a gathering of ridicule. You know, just to go through all of that trouble so that we can get attention, or, even better, to convert non-Christians to the light.

Oh, this has just been bunches of fun while trying to relate an unrelated topic to relatives whose relationships are really stressed because they can't relate even if they wanted to reach out and rub the relation of the related message right onto their ribs! Did I mention, **relate**?

This isn't easy, not in the slightest, yet I wouldn't trade what happened to me for the world. I'm in "the know" now, and I wish all who could see knew not what the world shows to know about what's hidden in "the know". Okay, enough with the riddles, but I hope you know what I mean (I had to throw one last "know" in there.).

Although I believe all people have the access to gain insight from what some might call "holy visions", I know that most will feel this is still unreachable. But as I've mentioned before, our dreams are not to be so easily doubted and tossed aside. If most people would take a minute to analyze some of the dreams that have stayed with them for a lifetime, a message from elsewhere might be found. It's important also to note that Jesus doesn't just come in dreams, as with my last encounter with Him and the one I'm about to mention.

I've even learned that it doesn't matter about a person's background or whether or not a Jesus encounter is possible. Imagine having a whole different religious upbringing where you specifically are taught that Jesus was not the Messiah the world had been waiting for.

This is the story of one Jewish man's encounter with Jesus and how it changed his perspective to include a new holy approach:

"I was sleeping in my bedroom when I felt that someone was standing at the doorway of my room. I sat up in bed to see this man smiling at me with a tremendous amount of care and love, which somehow touched me down to the soul of me.

"I never gave this man who stood before me the respect He deserved, being that I was Jewish. On the contrary, I laughed at people who claimed that a human being could be directly related to God.

"The irony was that as soon as He came, I knew who He was. I also knew we loved each other very much and that we were very good friends. It's a feeling I cannot describe with words.

"I know that I looked at this man directly, but I now only recall seeing His unnaturally blue eyes. I got up and walked towards Him, and He came further into the room and sat down on the floor with me.

"He started to talk to me about the reason He came to me, but for some reason, I was adamant to ask Him questions about my personal life. Again, I felt as if I was talking to my best friend in the world, and I just knew He would be able to help me with the problems that I was facing at the time. I also felt that since our friendship was so stable, that I had the right to ask Him anything I wanted, even if He had a different idea in mind.

"It was a strange feeling. Even though it is not the case, He came to me as an equal. It's like He didn't want people to see Him as someone better than themselves.

"So, when He began speaking, I asked Him a question — I don't recall what it was about. He answered me, and I don't remember the reply. He began again with His reasons for coming, and I asked yet another question. I don't recall that question or His answer, either.

"Then, as if to realize that I wasn't ready for what He needed to talk to me about, He began to stand. He seemed in a hurry to leave, and so I asked Him to stay since I wanted to continue speaking with Him.

"He then gave me the most satisfactory feeling of forgiveness, almost as if He felt He had come to me at the wrong time, that it wasn't my fault, and that I wasn't ready to hear Him.

"Jesus knew I wanted Him to stay, yet He started walking towards the doorway. I almost screamed for Him to stay and squeezed one more question in that I do remember. I asked Him what I should do regarding a critical problem I was having with my sister.

"Jesus smiled at my last question, but did not answer me. He soon faded away right before my eyes, and I was surprised that He had no answer. In fact, that whole part of the experience puzzled me the most. It was the only question that I recalled, and the only thing He didn't try to answer.

"Soon after He left, I felt sad for being so obsessed with my own worries and not having been willing to listen to Him. I still hope to see Him again one day and to behave better.

"A few days later, I was driving my car with the circumstance concerning my sister still on my mind. I'd written a letter to address my concern to her and was about to mail it off to her while I took a different route than usual. The thought of my seeing Jesus then entered my mind, and I thought again how He had never answered my last question.

"Then I realized, as I looked at the letter in my hand, that I was answering the question myself. I glanced directly ahead of me, and there, on a large church window, was the largest spectacle of colored glass, depicting Jesus with a huge smile on His face. It felt as if He was smiling at me, and it was nearly more striking for me that I saw His image at that exact moment than when I saw Him in my room! I never really looked much at churches, and I never noticed this one before. It just seemed like I saw Him at the right time, and it felt as if He was saying that He wouldn't leave me without an answer, but that Jesus helped me with it all along.

"Now when people like to make the assumption that just because I'm Jewish I must not be into Jesus, I like to be quite honest about Him and say, 'Hey, Jesus is my friend, too!' "

I think that's an awesome story, and such an honest one from someone that I personally know. I've had to leave some elements out, so as to protect the identity of my friend, per his request. But trust me when I say that I was truly stunned to hear this story coming from him, and it's been a treat to be able to talk to him about our life-changing encounters. As with my last encounter with Jesus, my friend related that this encounter was not a dream in any sense but a fully physical encounter with the Son of God.

God speaks to all of us in different ways, and one thing I have learned through all of my otherworldly outlets is that nothing is a coincidence. Things don't just pop into your head, or even into your life, for no apparent reason. There's always something there for you to decipher. Not all things are so easily understood initially, but eventually some purpose will come forward from what might have transpired.

Dreams provide a way we can learn more about ourselves and spirits, but we can also learn from our everyday lives. There are so many instances which come and go before our eyes all of the time that we can draw from. It doesn't matter how silly our matters can be or how catastrophic, either. Meaning can be found if we look at them the right way, and I try to do this for myself, too.

Just for the heck of it, I'll throw some instances out there on how to better look at our lives and occurrences: Say you bump into someone at a supermarket. Fast forward two years and you married that person, only to quickly divorce them. Was that whole crappy relationship really necessary?

Then there's the one time that you reached to grab your purse quickly, but in your scurry you snapped your expensive fingernail — the one you just had glued on that day. What was the purpose in that?

How about being talked into hanging out with your friends at a nightclub and someone else gets into a fight, a weapon is pulled, and you are severely hurt. Give me a break here!

Then there's your child, who slips and falls and is run over by her school bus, paralyzing her in the process. This is just a pain-filled incident where no outright purpose can be found.

Are all of these things just coincidence, or was it their time to happen? Some of these events might seem like extreme cases, but they could easily have happened to someone at some time. Just as these events come to pass, so do our dreams and meanings come if we let them, or so I've now learned. Sometimes in the face of bewilderment or trauma, it's as if we don't want to find any meaning to what happens in our lives. I believe it's because we are pigheaded, where often our mysterious events are left unresolved. We humans have this rare gift of allowing our troubles to sink to the bottom of our own oceans, where we don't have to look at them anymore.

Personally, I like to put a bobber on my mysteries to let them float to the surface to see the light of day, so if something drifts by in the current, it might lend some insight on my mysterious event. Then I might find, yeah, I bumped into that man at a supermarket and married him, only to divorce him because he needed to grow up. But I got a wonderful son out of the relationship, a son who made the whole relationship worthwhile.

Then that time I reached for my purse, sent my nail flying through the air, and almost took my eye out, because I was in such a rush. It taught me patience. Taking ten seconds more to casually walk over and pick up my purse would have spared my pocketbook from paying for another visit to Mr. Lee's to have my nail replaced and polished (not to mention sparing my tire rim that I banged into the curb while parking at the appointment that I was in such in a rush for). I wasn't paying attention to how I parked because I was so peeved that I broke that nail in the first place.

How about getting injured at the nightclub that I was so close to not going to with my friends? I had a feeling in my gut not to go out that night, but I went against my instincts, and now I was in pain at the hospital. I promised myself I would never ignore my gut telling me not to go somewhere and would make an effort to reassure others to do the same. But I don't stop there. The fact that someone even had a weapon at the club rolls me into action to ensure tougher laws against people bringing weapons into a public gathering.

Then there's my innocent child who slips in the snow and the bus driver doesn't see her and she runs my daughter over. Where's the sense in that? I don't want to look, but what could have been the purpose of this tragedy? My heart hurts all the time, but I didn't always give of myself to my daughter when she was fine. I was always too busy, or there was always tomorrow we could do the mother and daughter thing. Tomorrow never came, and I promised myself that I would take the time from now on with her.

Immediately following this tragedy, bus drivers in the area are re-trained to count the children who leave their bus to make certain that they indeed pass by before they pull away. This small act spares the lives of countless numbers of children and might spark other parents to be grateful for the time they share with their own children.

Nothing is wasted. There is always a reason why things happen as they do — always. These are just happenstance or make-believe instances, but it's everyone's story, and these things do happen. Thoughts, happenings, situations, dreams, and so much more come to us every day to take lessons from, and to analyze. They might not always be directly happening to us, but we can learn from them just the same, to grow with.

With dreams and our sleeping hours, maybe you felt you woke up to a bright light in your room at night. Maybe you had a dream where a stranger told you something of importance about yourself, or simply, "Everything will be alright." Perhaps a departed loved one came to you in your sleep, even if they had nothing to say, and you felt comforted by their presence. Perhaps you, too, saw people in your dreams with robes on, showing you different paths and teaching you better ways of living spiritually.

Little mysteries to bigger mysteries, we all have had them, of this I'm sure. But what we choose to retain as a part of our lives is the key, no matter how strange. I know how people think, because I happen to be a "people" too. Upon waking up, I would dismiss some of my experiences as being related to something I ate before going to bed. Better yet, I just must have had a very active imagination to come up with some of these whacked out "dreams" of mine.

But there came a time when I couldn't keep up the charade anymore. It took me time to think back about how, as a child, I would have dreams of the spiritual kind, and I didn't have any pre-judgments about them. I just accepted them for what they were. It seemed natural to allow understanding of my spiritual connection and that I was getting messages to interpret. Many of these dreams have stayed with me all of my life, and I consider myself as someone with less than average memory, so these dreams had to be something else for me to recall.

Trotting down memory lane once again, there was one dream in particular that still stirs and sometimes disturbs me. I was in the 5th grade, about ten years old, and living in the boonies on Milwaukee's Northwest side. We didn't have many neighbors who had kids, and those who did weren't very close in age to my younger sister and I, who was about eight at the time. We really loved playing with this young kid by the name of Michael, who was about six years old and lived across the way from us. He was too young to come over by our house alone, so if we played with him, it was usually at school and only rarely by his house.

One night I had a dream that I was walking down the block from my house and heard cries coming from a manhole in the street. I got up close to it, peered through one of the small openings in the lid, and asked who it was and what had happened.

As I looked, I could see that it was Michael. He recognized me and asked for my help to get him out of this peculiar situation. I told him I would run to my parents for help and not to worry, but when I got to my house, it was empty. So I grabbed a crowbar on my own and quickly ran back to where Michael was.

I was just about to pry the manhole open when I heard Michael's cries come from another manhole behind me. I looked in puzzlement, because that manhole hadn't been there before, but I still went over quickly to the other one. I asked Michael why he'd moved to this manhole, and he told me, more pointedly this time, to just open the lid. I couldn't see down this lid with no holes, and I felt something wasn't right, but I opened it anyway.

As soon as the lid came off, out of the hole came some kind of creature that I could only equate as being the devil. The creature laughed and thanked me for unleashing him unto the Earth. My thoughts went back to my friend, Michael, and my heart sank, as I realized this creature must have killed him or left him trapped under the pavement.

The creature then took a step toward me and tossed me into a nearby weeded lot, as he proceeded to wreak havoc on the world. I felt that this demon thought I was dead by him merely touching me, so I closed my eyes to let him continue to believe this. I planned on waiting until the creature walked by, and with my crowbar still in hand, I planned on going to the manhole to see if I could rescue my friend. As I lay there, feeling that I was perfectly fine physically, my soul slowly left my body and rose up into the air.

I soon found myself in a cloud-filled place, where many people walked around in robes, including myself. There were rows of people lined up and sitting on the floor in groups. I immediately knew these were families sitting together, and I recognized my own family and joined them. As soon as I stood with my parents and siblings, I allowed my mind to take in what had happened.

Somehow the creature had succeeded in kicking all the souls off the planet, and that all of our souls had accumulated in this place.

I hoped no one had suffered, since what had happened to me didn't hurt. Then I noticed that I didn't see one of my siblings with us. I wondered where my sibling was when my parents directed my eight-year-old sister and I to be seen by someone or something.

My parents told us to just go as we were, that our heads were to be kept down and our souls humbled. My sister went ahead of me, as I continued to talk to my parents, when suddenly we heard a loud crashing noise, as if glass was shattering everywhere. We all looked at each other in horror, thinking my sister did not make it, only to see her walking toward us, perfectly fine and smiling.

Then, it was my turn, and I walked away, wondering what mystery I was about to meet. I came to an opening in this endless area we were all in, as if there was an invisible room that we all recognized to be there, but which took up no space. Some robed men and women stood at the entrance, as if to be conversing on who entered this place. I looked up at them as I passed by at about eye level to their torsos and then put my head down as instructed by my parents. I ventured into this short tunnel and knelt there on the cloudy floor.

My head was still bowed, when an immensely bright light came from above my head. I closed my eyes tight, and I struggled with this sudden urge to look up into this light, which was against what I was told and knew not to do if I wanted to survive. I rolled wildly on the ground, and at times I was facing up toward the light, but I never opened my eyes. My body screamed to let my eyes look at the source of the light, but my soul held on and fought for strength against my body's will. I felt I was being scanned and then tempted to see my reaction, to see if I could remain loyal to my conviction and do what I was told.

The struggle was fierce, but I held on. Suddenly, the light stopped and the room grew dim. I remained on my back, exhausted and with my eyes pinched closed. I took my time opening my eyes and getting to my feet. Then, I slowly wandered to the end of the tunnel.

Upon exiting the opening, I walked toward my parents, who had proud smiles on their faces to see me "pass". Still, I felt somewhat ashamed that it had been so hard for me not to give in to my temptation, and I wondered if it was as hard for everyone else.

Ashamed, I kept my head down for a bit, then again I thought about my missing sibling. I quickly looked around but still couldn't find her, and I hoped that her soul would somehow still meet with ours. I gazed around this open space with souls who were so content, yet waiting, and I felt the same. I didn't feel I had brought this wrath of the devil upon any of us — it felt more like we had all contributed to what had happened by unleashing the dark side with our negative acts and by not trusting our instincts.

By some miracle, we had all still managed to get to this place, and were accepted and "passed" to be here.

I didn't wake up immediately from this vision, as if it were a dream. I awoke the next morning and felt I had gotten a message from God. I didn't try to put my vision through a societal filter that was taught to me about how absurd it was to think I could ever actually experience such a thing. I slapped on an outfit, ran to my bus stop, sat in class, swung my legs back and forth, and thought about the neat lesson God showed me in my vision.

I knew that I had been fooled by the devil, and that I should have trusted myself when I saw that there were two manholes and that Michael had moved to the other one. I knew he wouldn't have moved, but I went against my better judgment, and, lo' and behold, it was the devil! Dumb, dumb, dumb! I figured, "Oh, well, I'll know better next time not to take someone's word for things like that, but to trust my feelings first."

I was a kid, and I took the lesson to heart. But as adults, we think of all the reasons why we are nuts to even think anything about a "silly old dream". Well, if a person cannot accept the messages that come to them, at least be open to hear another person's experiences. If you don't trust your own mind in being sane enough to receive messages, maybe you'll take the word of your mother, brothers, sisters, or friends.

I admit that I haven't shared this above vision with too many people, just because it was so long ago, and I'd already learned my lesson in trusting my gut on what stands before me as being good or not. But, if it adds to helping other people understand that our life lessons come from all sorts of outlets, then I know it was good to share it. Keeping anything to myself that might help another person is a silly thought in general, and that goes for all of us.

If we cared less about the ridicule we might receive for speaking about something different from societal norms, then this might be a more spiritually evolved place. Yet, we all seem to let the masses rule us.

"If you see a sign, take it in, find some meaning in it, and try to share what you have found." That's my motto. If a person speaks from the heart, it should be easily recognized as being the truth by those who needed to hear the message in the first place.

CHAPTER

9

CHANGING DESTINY

Why does a chapter like this one fit into this book? I'm not asking you, I'm wondering myself. I had to put it in for some reason, so I did. I don't always know why I write what I write until it's written, so I'm going to see where this one leads me.

Hmm, I feel a bit preachy for some reason.

Well, the first thing that came into my head is the question about there even being a destiny. Some would argue that everything in this life has been handwritten by God to happen as He planned it. Then there's this thing about having freewill to choose to work *for* and *with* God, or not. How can they both exist simultaneously, or does destiny only work one way and only for some things?

Like the creation of the universe; God planned that. How about my tripping on my own shoelaces because I decided it wasn't important to tie them until I met with an untimely trip down the stairs? I'm guessing that this example was not destiny but my own freewill to decide to be stupid.

It's been said that if you grow up where your parents are associated more to one political party, you, too, will most likely have an affinity toward that party. This sort of thing is also said in relation to other interests which your parents pursue, that odds are you will lean in their direction, as well. For instance if your parents were Catholic, you are more likely to identify as such. If your parents went to college, you, too, may seek a higher education.

There's a cycle and rhythm to these sorts of traditions and habits, but they can be broken, thus changing what many might call a kind of destiny. No, it's not set in stone to be one way over another just because your folks are, and this needs to be realized for a lot of things in our lives in general. I wish everyone could say this together with me, "We can change!"

Right when I typed that, I imagined a motivational speaker at the podium of a large room saying those words for a get-rich quick money scheme. But these words are so very true, and they need to be brought right up to your belly, digested through the skin, and into your gut. There can be no savoring it in your mouth to be judged for taste and if it suits you, or it goes down your food pipe only to be thrust back up from acid reflux.

Let it sink in that we can control our destiny. Limits do exist, of course, because I'm a firm believer that some things are destined to happen and it is just a matter of time before they do. But who we are as individuals is all subjective, and we have room for tons of growth. I can't think of any other reason for my being here on this planet than to grow and learn spiritually and mindfully. If my life was all planned out of my control to happen at another's will, then there would be no reason for my coming here. I would be able to look it up in a heavenly crystal ball, see what happens to me, and probably find it boring, since I would know what the conclusion would be.

Ever have someone tell you how a movie was going to end, and it made you not want to go see it since you knew what was going to happen? If you can see your answer as being a big-fat "yes", then do you think God would spoil it for us to live like puppets with all the characters and events planned out in our lives? What about the possibility that we all chose what we were going to focus on in our lives, even before we arrived?

I am trying to go somewhere with all of these questions and babbling, and it's not an easy topic which I'm trying to tackle. I believe all of us do choose our destiny as we go along in this life, and perhaps even beyond that. Meeting Jesus was an incredible experience for me which helped bring so many puzzle pieces together in my mind, including one huge chunk.

There is yet another incident which happened to me which I was more than reluctant to put in this book (only because this book is about Jesus and not me, directly). But through the process of putting this all down on paper and always asking questions about where people are in understanding the spiritual world, I knew I would have to include this information at some point.

People seem to be able to relate to another person's plight as more than something they deem unreachable, so I'm hoping my personal story will bring more understanding. It's also my hope that this tidbit I'm about to share will bring more answers to the "Why me personally?" question I posed in the previous chapter.

Whenever I get sad about how hard it can be to get some enlightening information to people, or when people ask why I was lucky enough to see Him, in a sense, I do know why I'm in the situation which I find myself. Now, what I'm going to talk about doesn't make me feel special, or better. But can I say that I might be a little *different* than the next person? I *can* say that something is up with me, but only in the sense that I have recollections of some instances before I was born.

That wasn't a typo. I said "before" birth and having "recollections". Right now, I'm wondering how I can get out of putting down the whole thing which I'm talking about so I don't come off as being too strange, but, then again, this entire book is already off the hook of what might be considered normal. What the heck, you knew what you were getting yourself into by looking at this book, so I won't make any apologies.

Can you tell I'm trying to talk myself through this? I'll just spit it out now.

It was some time in May of 1997, on the second Tuesday of that month. It was a date I never looked up to keep in mind. I figured it was more important to know that it did happen, more than exactly when it happened. That's something to keep in mind when it comes to trying to define or confine everything that has no direct definition.

I was living with a good friend I'll just call Samantha, while attending college in Milwaukee. She and I had our share of strange happenings in our apartment which included seeing strange things together and independently from one another. In fact, on this particular day, she and I had just finished discussing an odd experience, when I stood up from my purple futon to walk toward the bathroom.

What happened next is as much of a mystery to me as anyone, because I have no idea why this came to me — and nothing like this has ever come close to happening to me again. Everything I know on how to explain a process or occurrence just escapes me when it comes to this experience. There is no certain answer or definition to what happened and what I saw.

All I can say is, after I stood up, I took a few steps toward the bathroom. Then while still chatting with Samantha, my vision went elsewhere, plain and simple.

I suddenly found myself gazing on a scene in space, looking among stars much larger than I had ever seen. Somehow, I knew I was looking at the Center of the Universe, almost as if it resonated within me to know that. There, in the middle of this beautiful scene in space, was a massive spinning light. It looked much like the sun, but the light spun clockwise, and there were trillions of smaller lights that made up the full mass of the spinning light.

Upon a closer look, I knew that these smaller lights in this gathering were all individual souls. Trillions upon trillions of souls were in what I tend to now call a "Love Soup" of souls. Then, I found myself in this Love Soup, among the souls, and

I experienced a wonderful exchange of information. Thoughts, ideas, decisions, and even goals passed through the light on what needed to be done. As the thoughts came by, each soul gave their opinion on it, and it somehow went to the center of the light and became one thought.

A thought came by that asked for a volunteer, a simple request that had a lot of responsibilities attached to it. My soul contributed to the thought in agreeing that I would go, and before I knew it, I was being sent out of the massive light in an instant! The feeling of anxiety from being detached from this Love Soup is nothing I can explain. I felt my soul screaming out from the heavy sorrow of leaving, and in my true lump of translated emotions, I yelled, "I take it back!"

That's not me trying to be cute, either. I really screamed throughout my very being that I didn't want to leave the light and the *Love* behind. If I could have dug my nails into the walls of space, I would have left a bigger mess than the Milky Way behind me!

In the middle of all of this reflection time, I was still standing in the middle of my living room, while Samantha was watching me standing there, and I was saying over and over, "Whoa, whoa, whoa!"

Samantha asked, "What's wrong?"

I soon sat down, now back from whatever had just happened to me. "How could I forget? How could I forget?" I kept repeating over and over adamantly.

"Forget what?" Samantha inquired.

"Who I am!" I asserted.

Samantha, of course, was beyond puzzled. Heck, *I* was puzzled about what had just happened. I began telling her of my visual trip of the scene in space, when I remembered, "The Source! That was the name of the light, the place I saw!"

I knew this place as if it was my old backyard. It was all so familiar to me, and it just baffled me how I knew all that I did.

"It was like my memory of this place was sitting right out in front of my forehead, and they let me have it for only a minute!" I explained to Samantha.

Exactly who "they" were I don't know, but something had to help me in recalling this place. To say that what I saw was a recollection was the best way to describe it, too. It just felt like a time of remembrance for me.

As I continued to explain to Samantha all that I had seen, I suddenly remembered seeing, at the upper-left of The Source, a red spinning mass of light. Somehow, I just knew this place was where everything and anything that has ever happened anywhere gets stored. It was very much like a library of knowledge and record.

I have since heard other people talk about a place like this library, and some have referred to it as being something called the Akashic records (A theosophical term referring to a universal filing system which records every occurring thought, word, and action). Whatever names people want to place on such things, I have no idea. All I know is that some things exist without a title and still exist. I am also not into the New-Age scene where people believe we are all individual gods and Jesus was just a soul that recalled more than the next soul.

I do know, however, that this place and center I know to be called The Source was the beginning of all beginnings, and that I somehow remembered my beginning. In recalling all that I did, I felt ashamed that I had let petty things in my life grab my attention and focus. I felt I should have been able to recall who I was and why I came here so I could have avoided so many unnecessary troubles. For me, it was like forgetting that my first name is "Heidi", something that is so instilled in me that it would seem silly to forget that. Yet, here, I had forgotten the very fabric of my being and my decision to come here to help.

Yes, there was something else I had recalled, as well. When the thought passed by for a volunteer, it was for an assignment to come and be born here to somehow help in the coming times.

Ha! Again I laugh at what people must think in reading this, *What the heck is she talking about? Just another loony needing to be cornered and hog-tied?*

With my first book, I wrote about what I felt people thought of, as well, in reading what they did. One person in particular suggested that when I put thoughts like that on paper, it looked as if I doubted myself and left a question in the reader's mind. Well, you know what; it's called, "Keeping it Real!"

Lord knows that I live and breathe like everyone else, and believe it or not, I socialize with people, too. So, yeah, I have a tendency to know what people might think when they hear things that are a bit off the beaten path. But either way, I cannot help but write what I know or have experienced, even against the scrutiny that I'm sure will come.

Oh, well... I have only one true judge to whom I must answer, and He's not sitting on the bench in front of me — just yet!

Now, where was I?

Oh, yeah! I was talking about recalling that I had come here to help in the coming times. What does that mean, the political crap times, war times, Day Light Savings Time, or the end times? I like to think of this time as the "Time of Change" times.

I personally used to think that these times were indeed the end times, and I am still not sure that we are not in those times. In fact, there are a ton of signs that I have been taught to be made aware of that point to our being in the last years on this planet. But I have been reminded in more ways than I can count that no one knows when that end time will occur. Again, some things are destined to happen, but it's always just a matter of time *when* that will be.

While I was recounting to Samantha about what I saw, I immediately felt that what I remembered was way too important to stall on. I talked to her insistently that I needed to drop out

84

of college so I could get right on top of doing what I recalled I needed to do. I remembered that when I left this Source, I went to be taught about what I needed to help with, and how. Whatever I learned there didn't compare to the textbook education I was taking in college. It all just felt like a waste of time, and I felt I had done enough of that by not remembering this other purpose for so long.

With the encouragement of friends, near and far, I remained in college to get this little piece of paper that spells credibility to some people. I don't feel any more credible or different by saying that I have a Bachelor of Science Degree behind me and am now a certified occupational therapist, licensed and registered. But some of you are nodding your heads, saying that it does make a difference, so this degree is for you. How do you like it? Is it all you ever thought it would be?

I have yet to make any good use of my lovely degree since I dropped it all to pursue matters of the soul, or at least since I've written this book. Thinking on how there's a reason for everything, I did need college to help with my writing skills on a lot of levels. Aside from taking English courses, I had a lot of essays to write, and I learned to do them quickly. I should say — supernaturally fast. Imagine coming into class and being told that the paper you forgot to write is due and excusing yourself to go back home to get it. But what I actually did when this happened to me was to go to the writing center on campus, spit out a fast draft, print it, and turn it in! So, although I saw no need for college while getting focused on my more spiritual matters, it helped in my learning how to get a message across.

From the beginning of my recalling who I was and my purpose, the biggest challenge was in wanting to remain here on this fluffy blue planet. Not that I wanted to die or anything; I was just so anxious to see this thing through so I could go back "Home".

Seeing that spinning light in space resonated within me and left me yearning to return to it like no other. I had no doubt in my mind that what I had witnessed was true and that I had agreed to come here. People can make their psychic predictions or wild guesses about what their purpose in life is and what they need to do to change their direction, but there is nothing quite like knowing for yourself and remembering all that you need to know. You can doubt what another person tells you about yourself, but you cannot lie to yourself and question your own memories.

I *had* made an agreement, and I knew it to be true. It was nothing that I could tell too many friends, or even tell my family about remembering things before I was born. How on Earth does that sound to say to anyone? So, all I could do was keep it among certain friends who had also experienced some of the stranger things in life and hope for the best.

To answer the question of why I got the chance to meet Jesus, I can say, to a certain extent, that I do know now. But to say I knew I would meet Him, heck no! There was nothing in my psyche that even hinted to truly knowing He was For Real.

Jesus gave me a wonderful wake-up call, and changed my destiny of knowledge in matters of the spirit. To think that at one time I felt so certain that I knew nearly all that was necessary to know when it came to soul issues concerning myself. I mean, here I had recalled coming from the Light of God and my whole life purpose, so I thought. But I was way wrong, and I didn't (and still don't) have the full picture of all that goes along with this life.

I don't know how I intended to do anything meaningful in my moment of wanting to drop everything to do this "mission" which I had recalled from the light. I just felt like I had to get busy and do something to wake folks up to their spirits, but the spirit of Jesus was missing in me — at least I thought it was. But He was there all along. Knowing Him, He was probably shaking His head and laughing at my silliness in forgetting His guidance being there, showing me the way.

Even upon seeing Him the couple of times I did, I thought I could go and start flapping my gums in knowledge of what His

Presence was all about. I wanted to talk about what His Purpose was and all that He could do, and how people needed to know that He was For Real. I could share some things for certain, but I still wasn't fully grasping what He was all about.

I had a loose knowledge about the Bible, and I'm still no expert on it. I'm just not the type to memorize tons of Scriptures so I can quote my thoughts out.

Some people thought that since I had seen Jesus, I would start reading the Bible religiously. I did pick it up now and then, but I felt it was more important to see how other people felt about Jesus and God in general. It seemed more essential to see if people were aware of Jesus and what they thought about the possibility of His role and the chances of His returning — and what that might mean. Also, I was plain curious to see if people felt they could bear knowing that if He did return and Him being who He was said to be in the Bible, would they feel safe and personally saved?

For the most part, people seemed to think of Him as the Son of God, but for some reason, those words didn't seem to truly hit home with them.

"Son of God." To have a title like that is absolutely huge. You can't say those words as if you are ordering a Big Mac with a large order of French fries. Jesus isn't a side dish to fill up the rest of your appetite. He is a part of the Whole of God. Jesus, the Son, an Extension of God, a Piece of the Pie, just as we carry the same DNA and traits of our parents, so does He. He is capable of doing similar acts as His Father and resembling Him as we do our parents. He is connected to the whole with a bond beyond comprehension and is together at the same time in a Trinity of the Father, Son, and Holy Spirit.

I don't know why I needed to get into details on this, but it seemed to be of importance. Too many people like to focus on details, as if it will help make their aim for reaching God clearer so they can bypass that Jesus guy. We aren't shooting darts here. Our hearts can aim for tons of targets all at the same time, with just a glimpse. That was another lesson I learned that I will be talking about later — on how our prayers can work.

Our thoughts don't have to be so darn pointed to have them reach their destiny, and Jesus doesn't have to be so strangled to be defined. I had already met Him twice and thought I was so blessed and knew so much to share with others, but I hadn't even scratched the surface of who He is. There were more lessons to be learned. I needed to know what He was truly about and how He felt.

Jesus would come another time and share a part of Himself with me, and I am shocked that I could even handle what He had in store for me. The mind is a powerful thing, and the soul is even stronger. Jesus is a special soul to endure all that He has, and you think He had it rough when He suffered for all of our sins on the cross? You have no idea what He endures now in seeing all of the mess we have gotten ourselves into today.

10

THE BURNING HEART

I had a hard time understanding why people, including myself, often spent too much time on issues that really didn't matter in the long run to our spiritual lives. It just seemed I was always hearing a story of someone talking about someone else because their eyebrows were unkempt. Or another person looked at someone strange, which provoked a fight somewhere. Then there's the person not speaking to their brother for years because he borrowed a camera that he never returned, minor glitches that attract such big flaws out of us.

I had gotten the chance to see outside of this world and take into perspective how petty some of our squabbles are, yet I still slipped and participated in them myself. It was easy for me to see how stupid they were, and I got angry at myself and others for letting these silly barriers interfere with daily growth. I felt powerless and wanted to find a way to let the errors of my ways sink into my skull so I could get it into other people's skulls, too.

Of course, it's easier to see the faults in others than in ourselves, so I had this wishful thinking in my head in wanting to know the hearts of people. I often met with people who never were what they appeared to be, whether they were just negative people or negativity in sheep's clothing. I was tired of being deceived, and I was fed up with not knowing who to trust and where their heart was. So, of course, I prayed on this notion and wondered how I could better understand people and their prerogatives.

The new millennium had come and passed, and it was now February of 2000. February is a cold and bitter month in Wisconsin, where winter gets in its last licks with snow and harsh winds. I usually didn't sleep with anything less than thick socks, sweat pants, and a T-shirt with a sweatshirt on top. Then, on my bed was a set of sheets, an underlying fuzzy blanket, and a thick comforter covered by a handmade crocheted bedspread. I didn't play around when it came to battling the cold, whether I was conscious or not.

This night I went to bed as usual and went through one of the longest nights of my life. The next morning I awoke cautiously and prayed aloud, "Take it away, please! Take it away!"

From what I recalled, I had a waking-dream of talking with someone about wanting to know the hearts of people. I was in some kind of lighted place with an indistinguishable structure while I discussed the implications of what I was asking. I expressed how tired I was of deceitful people and couldn't see how I was to help with anything if I did not even understand those around me.

I felt that the entity I was speaking to thought this over and decided to let me see for myself what I was really asking. The next thing I knew, I was seeing people in their everyday lives, going about their business. Then, like big gaping wounds, their thoughts and emotions poured out of them, screaming my way.

I felt I put my hands over my ethereal ears and looked at those people in horror with the thoughts they had and negative vibes. There was so little harmony and contentment; people were confused and lost with so much about themselves and goals. Not one person smiled from the inside out, only surface smiles that had so much pain they never let go of. Hearts were drenched in agony, and questions about their meaning for living just ached out of their very being.

I traveled and was met with more of the same. It seemed that sometimes the souls of people were brought closer to me, instead of my going to them, so that I might experience a wide range of emotions. It was as if certain selections of people showed varying degrees of discontentment and lack of direction, and I had to be sure to experience the varieties that were out there.

I recalled allowing my eyes, ears, and soul to take everything in, and I just looked on with shock and sadness over their pain. I had no idea why people reacted the way that they did, but I knew that because their own souls were being ignored, they also ignored the feelings and condition of other people's souls. People could hardly understand themselves, let alone try to be fully considerate of anyone else.

I now understand that, for the most part, people are cordial and polite in front of others. But when it comes to peeling back our manners and revealing our souls, there are raw feelings of everything imaginable, with no boundaries. This hole in our face allows us to do and speak of rotten things with little regard for others and participate in more than petty squabbles.

I saw this and realized what a mistake I had made in asking for this gift of knowing the true hearts of men.

It wasn't pretty, and I didn't want any part of it, so at the first sign of a break from feeling all this pain from others, I asked for it to be taken away. Almost instantly the vision started to fade, and I awoke with this distinct feeling that there was a chance this gift still lingered.

I sat up in bed and wondered cautiously if I could still "feel" people. It was already morning, so I freshened myself up in the bathroom and grabbed a bowl for cereal. I knew that my one way of knowing if this "gift" had gone away was to see Samantha, who hadn't stirred yet from bed.

I slurped down mouthfuls of cereal and milk as I waited with a strained look on my face, dreading the thought that any gift like that could hang on me.

I finished eating. Samantha awoke and swaggered my way in a morning slumber. I looked up and smiled. I could have hugged her for being as shallow as the wall beside me!

Nothing stuck with me, and I was thankful for that and thanked God, too. I was as thick-headed as a tree stump when it came to understanding how anyone felt and wondered why I had even got the chance to feel such a thing. I thought it might all be just a wild notion I had and left it at that for about five minutes. I knew how my so-called "dreams" worked and that they were not always simple dreams. Something was trying to get a message to me, and I wasn't sure how or why. Okay, so I had asked to know, but who would think that my request would go so far, if at all?

Some time in March of 2000 my question about this riddle would be answered. March isn't the friendliest of months, as far as the weather goes, so I didn't falter in keeping my mound of blankets and nighttime clothing. I was all snuggled under my blankets and sound asleep when I remember sitting up and taking in heaps of emotions from someone in my room.

As I propped myself up and lifted my eyes, I felt at ease, as I inherently began taking in the beautiful sight before me. There, standing behind a colorful array of flowers and decorations, much like an altar of offering, was Jesus! I could see the outline of His hair and body from the waist up standing behind this colorful mass, and it seemed that light came from behind Him, shadowing His face. It's kind of strange to think of His face being shadowed when I saw so many colors all around and could see His brown hair and white robe.

His Presence was undeniable, as before, and the recognition of it being Him, again, was immediate. From the area of His chest, a great light poured forward, as if He had rolled away His clothing to bare His Soul. His Heart singed mine with burning emotions. It tore my heart to see that He felt all that He did.

Strong, just absolutely heavy burdens flew from Him and into the air. I could feel His immense sorrow for all that was happening to the people, how sorry He felt for absolutely everything negative that was going on. I'm contemplating on trying to name some of the specific things He was feeling with this sorrow, but it is nearly impossible. It was the whole of the whole, anything and everything you could imagine that has gone wrong or has turned sour.

In His heart was the weight of the world and all that had gone bad on this planet since its creation. But the most pain I felt was for the souls. There was this immense, lost feeling. It was if the physical planet itself could be healed, but the people had to make an effort if they were to receive the same chance for healing.

The best way to describe this emotion coming from Him was just outright Empathy that was **so** strong it could engulf the whole universe. Pity, love, sympathy, patience, understanding, joy, compassion, wanting to take everyone into His arms to make it all better, this Son had it coming out of Him in just heaps!

I took it all in and fully understood . . . and cried. His second emotion which then flowed toward me was about change and how anxious He was for it to take place. Efforts needed to be made, and people needed to take the existence of their souls seriously. There were no words like you and I can speak coming from Him. Just raw emotions — and there was no mistaking what He was feeling.

He was anxious to return!

My heart was pulled so strongly, and I felt His yearning to return to finish what was started. I don't know what His plans are, how He is going to go about doing what He floated my way, but I do know He wasn't making light of His intentions of returning soon.

The man (the Son) was no joke, and I knew He had come to urge me into understanding what was at stake and maybe even help others to understand. I still have no crowning authority to say I know what is absolutely best for everyone. But what I feel is that people need to be brought into awareness and understand why they are in the rut they are in. Negativity exists in us and in our lives because we let it exist, but now it has grown so strong that there is no way we can handle it alone.

I feel that if we had all of the answers to our personal complications, we would have no complications. There would be peace around us and in us, yet it's not a part of our reality because it is so foreign to us now. Why don't we know peace fully if we are so capable of depending only on ourselves? Something is missing, and we know it.

We all search for this missing morsel by joining different groups and beliefs, hoping someone will suddenly tell us truths that we can make our own. In actuality, we already own the information but are reluctant to believe ourselves. I doubt that I could have the recollections of my existence before being born here, had it not already been in me to recall.

I know that it's not an easy task to even contemplate recalling our pre-birth lives, and I would never suggest someone aim for that. What's important is to know that there is help, that there is a God, and that Jesus is right there next to Him. Meaning, He's always there and will be here sometime soon.

How soon? All I can say is, "Your guess is as good as mine." But when I look at my experiences and all of the visions people are having of Him more recently, I would say that the time is near.

When Jesus came to me this time, He opened my soul to see and feel what it was He felt for everything and everyone on this planet, and it's something I will not forget. No words could suffice in what was relayed, and He had no words to give about how His burdens felt. He came as He left — a mystery to me. I never saw how He arrived in this instance, and I didn't see how He departed.

I awoke the next morning and things seemed completely normal, that is, until I went to work. It took time, but flashes of memory started coming back to me on what had taken place during the night. Something was different about this experience, because it wasn't outright in my memory, but parts of it began pulling up as the "gift" returned.

What I once thought to be much like a nightmare, where I could feel the hearts of men, slowly became a reality. It began immediately that first morning following this visit from Jesus. I had a feeling something had happened during the night, but I still wasn't sure what it was. I got ready for work and hopped into my rusty car to start my day off when something disturbing happened. Odd emotions started seeping into my car as I drove to work, and I wondered what was in the air that felt so different. I doubted that it could be what I thought it was, because it was much less intense than I remembered from my waking dream about the "gift".

I went into work, did my job, and wondered all day if I was feeling what I thought I was. As time passed and days turned into weeks, I remembered the whole picture of seeing Jesus in my bedroom. I later recalled more and more, as I developed my own sense of awareness and even a sense of other people's emotions.

The "gift" had indeed returned, but this time much more slowly. I eventually began to feel the pools of gaping wounds around me, but I learned to look at them differently and keep a safe distance.

I admit I was frightened at times that people might drop mini-bombs of emotions on me. But I swept my courage up, trotted onward, and kept in mind that all of these chump shots were manageable.

There were still times when I hung near folks who would have high emotions just jutting out from them, where they knocked me a couple of times.

For the most part, I was able to live out my days without thinking about this gift clinging to me. It was much easier in real life than in the dream I had of having this gift and the souls of people screaming out at me. In my day-to-day life, it was more like there was a strong emotion at the tip of someone's mind that jumped right off of them like a bad smell. It could be a positive or negative emotion; it didn't matter — if it was high on someone's mind, it came out.

I once told a friend of mine about this peculiar gift I had received after seeing Jesus this third time and how people needed to keep their emotions and souls in check. It had taken some time, but I learned that for us to find peace, we have to know our limits. Doctors know that too much stress on certain body parts wears those parts down. Too much junk in our systems wreak havoc everywhere in our body as well. People also know that stress works against us in trying to get any sleep or live healthy lives with each other.

Well, then, I think people need to treat their soul as another part of their being that needs tending and respect if they want it to survive, too. If a person keeps feeding their soul crap, it will work like crap and not grow. If you don't feed the right fertilizer for growth, negative things will clog up the soul. Better yet, as I told my friend, think of it as a finger joint. When people are out of control with their souls, it's like bending your finger all the way backwards, going beyond the joint's capability. This can't be allowed to happen if you don't want your finger to crack in two pieces.

Instead, let the finger go the allowable distance, the extent of the joint. As you relax your finger, it will eventually go back to its natural stage and curl comfortably under the palm of your hand, well protected.

When I've walked past or dealt with people and felt their emotions out of control, it felt like a bunch of snapped fingers crunching underneath my shoes! I've even told this same friend that it was almost rude to be throwing all of that around for someone who's sensitive to that stuff to step into. Because I've noticed that at times I get overloaded with what's reflected my way, and I display the same high emotions I run into, whether good or bad (which is something I'm still working on to not have as an excuse — oh, the humanity in me).

Our souls have limits, and we need to know them. The pain we allow them to endure only weakens who we are and increases the pain Jesus feels. There's strength in our being, and people need to stop doubting that very real, human potential. It's something to be reckoned with; otherwise we would already be a beaten and defeated race among the rotten scoundrels of our universe. Call them scoundrels, demons, darkness, Shadow People, negative aliens, or whatever; we all know what we mean. We can stand strong against the odds, and we need to know that and take it to heart fully.

Show Jesus that you got the message, so you can lessen His strain, and put a footprint or two in the sand next to His while on your life journey.

11

PICTURE PERFECT PRAYERS
OR PICTURE PRAYERS?

"I'll keep you in my prayers."
"Lord, take me up in our prayers."
"Let us pray."
"Pray for me."
"Pray to our Father."
What is with all this praying going on?

Some of us thrust our chins up toward the heavens with our hands outstretched to throw ourselves up for help from God, with solemn words and thoughts. We babble on and on about how we need help, all the while hoping we say the right words so as not to be disrespectful to our God so that He will smile at our manners and grant us what we ask.

Then there's the sign of respect others of us do in bowing our heads and cramming our chins into our chests with our eyes closed and rolling tight prayers about in our hearts and minds. With such dedication, such poise in our praying stance, God must surely be pleased. It is almost certain then that God will answer, because tradition has been followed to the millimeter on how to pray properly.

I used to think to myself, when I would pray with my head down, *Wow, I look just like my grandpa with that seriously strained look on my face and veins poking out my forehead and all. If this prayer doesn't work, nothing will, because I know I have it down to perfection!*

Soon after my mother's passing, my sister Michelle was the first to teach me and my younger sister Keisha how to pray each night. We were taught something about it in Sunday school at church, but nothing stuck in our minds until our sister came and made praying more personal. Michelle told us it was like saying hello to our mom whenever we missed her, and that it was always good to talk to God, too, since we were dropping by where He lived in Heaven as well. We were sure to let our sister know that we missed our dogs Buffy and Ling-Ling, too, who had run out of our yard and were presumed forever lost or dead. (Note: It was later rumored that "someone" saw to it that the dogs did some time at the dog pound, but I'm not pointing any fingers.)

Michelle assured us it was okay to say hi to the dogs, too, if they were in doggy heaven. So, after each of our prayers, we decided to dedicate a blown kiss for each individual that we missed.

Mom, Buffy, and Ling-Ling were never far from our minds for years, because we were certain to send them our thoughts with our kisses each night after a prayer. After several years, the meaning for the three kisses left my mind. It became a habit that after each prayer I was to give three kisses and a quick blow, as if to send them off to Heaven to reach their destiny. But I had left the destination for the kisses out of my mind, yet I still did the kisses anyway.

I was seven years old when I had been taught to pray that way, and I was a young adult before it dawned on me that I was still doing a child's prayer. I laughed at myself and couldn't believe that I had carried on giving kisses to my mom and dogs who had died so long ago. I didn't regret doing it, especially for my mom, but two Pekinese dogs, and one with a bad attitude?

99

It was more than ridiculous of me to think that I still did that, and I couldn't bring myself to ask my younger sister if she still did the same thing after all those years. To say the least, I felt a bit silly about my habit and wondered if I had been an actual queen of some country, if I might have made my praying style a law to subside its silliness. Making it law would have made my silly ideation of prayer to be the norm, because then everyone would be doing it — or else!

I knew there were other ways of praying, but I didn't feel like anything major was broken at the time, so why fix it? I would get my point across, and I did the form in which I was taught — close my eyes and put my hands together. What more needed to be done in speaking to God? Well, I knew I had to say at the end of each prayer, "In Jesus' name, amen."

My head knew why I had to, but my heart didn't know why I said that stuff at the end, yet I did it anyway. I followed it in tradition, as I'm sure a lot of us do without thinking that there could be other ways to show our good intentions in talking to God.

In thinking on how I did my prayers; they were so boring and rehearsed that I almost always fell asleep in the middle of them. I would usually be in bed already, and I'd put my hands together and begin my ramblings, "Oh, God (You have to say "Oh" just like your pastor does, of course.), please forgive my sins as I forgive others, and bless my parents and brothers and sisters — even the one I don't get along wi– ZZZZZ . . .."

I would always awake in horror an hour or more later, knowing I didn't finish my prayer and thinking that it didn't get heard at all because I hadn't put the finishing touches on it yet. "Uh... amen. Oh, did I mention the sister I didn't get along with?"

I would then smile to myself, thinking that I was successful in ultimately remembering to finish my prayer for that night. Falling asleep like a baby in peace was easy to do after that final "amen", because I felt like a dutiful worker of God, having remembered to think of Him at the end of my day.

As God as my witness, these nighttime prayers were my routine for years while growing up! They changed only slightly after I became an adult, and when I moved out of my folks' home, I just got to leave out of my prayers the part about my sister who I didn't get along with. I didn't always have the exact same worded ramblings, but, essentially, those were my prayers.

I haven't sat in to hear anyone else's prayer ramblings, but my guess is that most of us don't have a huge range of characters in our prayers. Hey, if you are one of the rare ones who do — good for you! I would think it to be a rarer occurrence to always have a broad scope of people in our prayers, although I fully hope I am wrong.

I wondered for years how I could spice up my prayers to keep myself conscious long enough to complete them. As a child, I felt guilty about this subject and wondered, even then, what I should do about these praying sleep attacks. It later dawned on me, *We pray during the daytime in church, so why can't I try to pray during the day?*

So I tried it. I actually began praying during the day as a teenager, but the bedtime prayers remained without much improvement. Praying during the day made for odd challenges, though, since I had little opportunity to be alone, and people could see that I was praying if I put my hands together. So I got "creative" and wondered if it was really necessary for the hand thing and decided I would have to make do without it.

Unbeknownst to myself, by doing this simple act, my prayers started to evolve. They became less formal, and almost more powerful, as if I were having something more like conversations with God. Sometimes I would look to the ceiling or the sky and just bop out something of concern in my head with words from my heart. It became a habit for me not to close my eyes when I did this, so people would not know I was praying.

I know why some people look up toward the sky or ceiling to pray, because they feel they are directing their thoughts to God in Heaven. For myself, I started looking up to the ceiling or sky in response to my time spent locked up in the bathroom while growing up.

If you are thinking that I'm referring to child abuse (the whole "being locked up in the bathroom" thing), you would have to take another guess.

My siblings, one in particular, had this "Let's gang up on Heidi!" mentality. I think it was a hobby or something, because I still see no rhyme or reason for it. So I took refuge in the room of the house with the only lock on the door.

In my long hours of sanctity locked in the bathroom (by my own will) to escape my siblings, there were three icons above the tub wall. One icon was of Jesus, the other Mary, and the centerpiece was a cross.

I would sit on the toilet while waiting for my parents to return and ask God why I was always in this predicament. I would turn my eyes upward and look into the face of Jesus, who had a crown of thorns and was fully painted in gold. I soon forgot the poundings on the bathroom door and remained entangled in prayer and peace in my heart. Even when my siblings would, at times, get the door open a crack to scream obscenities at me, I was so involved in thought and prayer that I didn't even hear them.

When my parents came home, sometimes I was so at peace I didn't even bother to mention my ordeal to them. I suppose the fact that I could be so calm was a combination of making peace within myself and knowing that I could only truly rely on God.

I knew there was nothing that would change my home life on the physical plane, so wanting to leave this life sometimes came to mind. I knew that was not the way out of anything, although I could hardly see how, a lot of the times. So I just kept the faith that God would somehow see me through it.

In the meantime, my daytime prayers started to have more meaning for me — they meant life. I don't know what was up with my nighttime prayers, though. I still did them and followed them blindly for years, and I figured I was good for keeping up with my prayers every night like that. I don't know why I didn't give my daytime prayers of conversation as much credit at the time, because they literally saved my mind and life.

At times my prayers of conversation were pushed, because I was desperate at the time, running from my siblings and into the bathroom. Other times, things were quite casual and natural as I would converse with God, usually while taking my long walks to work and home. Sometimes I would send a thought or two to God even when I took my usual seat upon the stool in the bathroom and glanced up at my old friend in gold on the wall. If you must know, yes, even when I contributed to the toilet, I could not help but look His way with a smile or thought. I didn't think God or Jesus would mind. I was still being positive and thinking good thoughts, so how could it hurt anything?

Gasp, drop your jaw, or whatever it is some of you formal folks might do. You can't tell me you haven't thought of God while on the pot at some time in your life. If you haven't, well then maybe you are not as devout as you thought, or just for the moment your focus was elsewhere. ☺

So, yeah, I've had my moments of being improper in the eyes of the church, as if any churches have eyes, anyway. If they did, they would have seen this coming, where God might be spoken to while out of perfect form. Yes, I know that Jesus even spoke of how to speak to His Father, but I don't recall His saying there was only one way of doing it.

All of this chatter on how I have personally evolved in my own praying, how it was taught to most of us in our lives, and what's proper, has led to something. At the time it happened, I didn't actively seek to receive what I did, but it was something I ached for and didn't even know I needed. Prayer had a simpler form that could give more power and meaning than what most of us ever knew. I wish I had known this prior to my own battles with prayer and taking time out for it, but everything comes in due time.

It was in April of 2000 that I had an incredible tidbit on prayers come my way by some unseen force. Again, I don't know why or how this strange piece of information came my way. All I know is that I got the message, and I am passing it on.

I was at a conference for the curious-minded that was held in a town nestled in the beautiful Ozark Mountains, where I would go almost yearly to hang out with other frequent visitors of the conference. We all had the general interest in hearing about news of the strange that our newscasters just so happened to censor and ignore our need to know about in our world. So, it was neat to meet other truth seekers and chat openly about oddities without some of the snickers you can get from other numbskull members of our society.

Being at this conference always gets my energies up and makes it hard for me to come down, even to let my body rest much. So, if there is ever a time when I have been afflicted with insomnia, it has been at this conference. This year in particular was really a high point where sleep had little part in it.

It was Friday afternoon — no, maybe it was Saturday. I really don't know what day it was since they started to blend together while I was there on this short weekend. I was with Jim, a person from the group of friends whom I came to the conference with. He and I were both keeping the same hectic pace during this conference, when we decided to take a nap in our multi-shared hotel room.

So, off we ventured. I hit my bed and he hit his, which was across from me. My reddened eyes closed, and I was off to La-La Land, or so I thought.

After what felt like five minutes of hard snoozing, I suddenly felt my mind and soul open up to "something" like an angel whispering in my ear, as I started to download information from afar. Then, pictures, serene images, and thoughts formed in my spiritual eye and mind, as if a lesson of some sort were being given. I felt myself nodding in response to what was being taught and shown to me in this spiritual classroom. Then, a promise was asked of me to share what I had seen, and I agreed.

Less than an hour passed, and I bolted upright in my bed and exclaimed, "Jim, they showed me something!"

Jim roused slowly and questioned what the heck I was talking about. I then began to tell him that something that I felt was an angel showed me how to pray. I was at a loss for words, but I did my best to sum up what I had just seen and learned. Jim seemed amused that I was so darned excited.

In this vision, almost as if in a haze of white and crystal blue light, I was immersed in the middle of knowing and seeing prayers. Although outright words didn't seem to be a part of the communication, words could be put to what was transmitted my way. I was shown people trying their best to formulate words to communicate what they needed of God in their prayers. I saw people's lips moving in quiet mumbles, bent knees, bowed heads, closed eyes, clasped fingers, and yes, even veins poking out of their foreheads in intensity!

The words that were being put together by these people in prayer were then shown to try to form a picture in my mind. Jumbled images like puzzle pieces and scattered thoughts floated before me, and I found it hard to relate one piece to the other. I looked at the mess and tried to understand what they each meant. It took some time, but I eventually began to feel what was meant by the words and intentions of the praying individual who had sent them.

I felt as if there was much work involved to find out such a simple fact of what was needed. For a millisecond or two, I wondered why I had seen such a thing, but then the answer came my way.

I was shown a life full of visuals — I don't know if it was my own life or everyone's. Events and concerns were met in this life, colors, pets, bills, schools, houses, and people were all a part of this existence. Then, pieces of this life were cut out from the scenes I saw and reassembled before me to one side. Feelings of intention, concern, and love seemed to come forward and hung to the other side of my view. Then suddenly, like putting glue on the back of a photo, the feelings sucked into the images, and they meshed before me as if they had never been separate. A feeling of "oneness" swept over me, like the images and their attached emotions were considered as one. They then quickly turned into a ball of spinning light and were sent forward in a flash to a destination where help would be lent to the asker — to God!

This lesson, without direct words, then guided me to practice this in my own life. I felt as if it was saying, "Take what you see in your own life, look at it, and put your feelings to what you have concerns about."

So I thought about the things I had concerns about and thought of my parents. I hoped they would remain healthy and happy for years to come. I then thought of my spiritual path and hoped that I was making the right decisions along the way.

In my head, I made up the visual of my parents and then thought of one of myself. Then, as if to take a snapshot photo, I captured those images in my mind. I thought of the feelings of intention I wanted associated with those visuals and attached them with my mental glue. I had my prayer package and focused these concerns toward God, and they were sent on their way with a closing of Jesus' name and amen.

I was thinking how fast and easy that was, when suddenly the lesson changed from no outright words to what seemed like direct words. It was hard to pinpoint, only because so much emotion came with all that was around me. These latter points were made so clear, though, that I feel they almost had to be sent to me in words to be sure I got it right in my human head so that I could get the message correctly to others.

"Words fall short of what is meant." Then another image of a person's life came forward with their feelings attached to it. "Prayer can be done this quickly; this is how we communicate."

It was then acknowledged that people needed to know this, and I promised I would share the information. I was more than ecstatic to do just that, being that I personally knew I had suffered by worrying and wondering if I was even praying in the right form and fashion. So, when I bolted up to tell Jim about what I had seen, I could hardly contain my excitement in telling him as fast as I could.

He and I were mentally crisp, although we'd had little sleep. Jim intently listened to my quick recounting, rolled back, and said, "Well, that makes sense."

I then rolled back on my bed and said, "Yeah, it does. I wonder why no one has ever thought of it."

It hit me that after all I had learned about God and Jesus, "Love" was their main message. But love is an intention, much more than the four-letter word. When you say you love someone, it means nothing if your actions don't show it. I am not saying that words have no intention behind them, especially while in prayer. It's just that mere words can fall far short of what is intended!

It seems as if I'm playing with words in what I'm trying to say, but it's all in truth, the truth! (Okay, that time I did a play on words just for fun, but I am sure you can see the difference.)

Our hearts and minds are more complicated and deeper than any word we can ever think up to define them. So much exists without words, and yet they still exist. Man has this habit of placing labels, such as naming newly discovered stars after themselves, so when we talk about that star, others will know what we are talking about.

For God, all you have to do is look at the star or point your heart that way and send Him your thought on it. No label needs to be given; just send Him a snapshot photo of your heart's intention, and there you have it — and so will He!

After being shown how to pray like this, I admit I felt a bit dumb for the entire human race for not figuring that out on our own. Although, since you can't make a buck out of praying, it should truly be no wonder why we never did. If it doesn't have its weight in gold, then it seems it's not worth the effort to share, according to our lovely race of beings.

Personally, I found this form of prayer to be worth more than anything physical that anyone could give me. I found peace of mind and soul in knowing I was communicating like the angels do. Would any one of us who believes in angels think that angels talk as we do?

Imagine Bob the angel needing some assistance from angel Karla. "Yeah, uh, Karla? You think you could drop by the Continent of Africa for a minute on your way to God? It seems the world thinks these folks are disposable and are letting them starve there. What's that? Yeah, we're taking names of those guilty on this, but the list is so big that I've run out of paper and was wondering if you could drop some off."

I highly doubt that they would be so basic with words. All that would be needed is a whispered thought, and the intention would be known amongst them. Imagine how much could be accomplished if we were all able to communicate in such a fashion.

I found that when I began praying this way, my thoughts got more precise and my intentions clearer. If I could have a friend lean into my thoughts, there would be no miscommunication and no room for misinterpretation. There would also be no rolling of eyes in boredom, because I found this communication to be swift, as well, where only a short time of focus was needed.

Not only was it fast to send out the thought in a flash of intention, I found that I was able to look into my heart and know myself better and know what I needed help with or wanted help for. I could think, in an instant, what I was most concerned with, what it looked like, who was ill, keeping my parents safe, child-abandoned television news, my hair is turning gray, pollution, what's that smell is, whose dog is lying in the street; I hope that doesn't leave a stain, where my keys are, how I will pay the bills; I need more tape on my car's bumper — it all could be packaged quickly into my Picture Prayers!

My prayers became complete, full, and not missing anything. Better yet, with everyone being in such a rush these days, time for praying was not even a factor. It especially isn't a factor for you now, either, since you know this information, too. Remember, with knowledge comes responsibility and liability.

I've got you thinking, haven't I? I knew that if I could share this prayer portion with people, no one would be able to say that their life was so full that they had no time for prayer. Remembering to pray is another story, but it is something that doesn't have to be rehearsed, either.

I found my most meaningful prayers to be in the light of day, right in the middle of doing something. It only took a few moments of focus and a lot of heart, and off my prayers would go, and my day would feel so much more complete. I would get all of my personal chores done, and on top of that, get in a quick chat with God.

Prayers became not a burden, but an asset.

Finally, there was true light that could be met at the end of my nights, if I chose to give a prayer before bed. Formalities were sometimes still practiced with my eyes closed and hands together, but they lessened in frequency. The best thing about that happening is that I knew it was okay for me to be looser in my prayer presentations. I knew it was okay for any and all people to form their prayers from their hearts as a source, with their mind used only as a guide.

It's been several years now since learning about "Picture Prayers", and I have only had the joy to share this with a few people who would listen. I knew the time to shine this on to others on a larger scale had not come yet.

I have a feeling this book will help get the message out. I wish I could have just sent the thought out if I knew there were receptors out there to catch it. For now, my written words, with huge chunks of intention behind them, will just have to suffice.

Tidbit: Due to the interest and importance, I expanded on this method of praying in my book named: **Picture Prayers***.*

12

THE THING WE WANT MOST

Praying, heck, having a faith of any kind is mostly done because of what? Now really think about this. What really guides most folks as individuals, and as a group, to be faithful to God?

It's called "Everlasting Life".

Through faith, people are hoping to reach this epiphany of the ultimate reward of living forever in some form. We see from our friends and family who have died before us that this life is pretty darned short and vulnerable. Then there's a rumor floating around that there's a fountain of youth, or better yet, everlasting life to be had. C'mon; you'd better believe we're all going to scramble for a way to find it!

We all want to know what package this eternal life comes in; what are the requirements to get it, and which button we need to push to trigger it. You come to the conclusion that you want this treat to life without suffering, but then you see there are a ton of avenues to take. You have the Christian, Jewish, Muslim, Buddhist, Voodoo, and all kinds of other faiths for you to take a peek at and see if any of them offers the way to everlasting life.

However, this seeking of a reward for doing something that is not truly of the heart should not be the reason for seeking truth.

Perhaps you have a fear of burning in a Hell-like place, where you are tortured for eternity, as is rumored by some faiths as punishment for not being a decent human being. Well, now that can be seen as a just cause for seeking out truth, but are you doing that just to save your own skin? What motivates people to look into these faiths, and does it count if you are looking into them for the wrong reasons?

I would gather that an all-seeing God would know your heart and your reasons for doing what you do, so you need to be true to yourself for your own reasons, because they will eventually be known to God.

There's this event which Christian's call "Judgment Day" that is to come when this world ends and all people are taken to be judged for the things they've done in their life (Note: Jews and Muslims also include something similar in their religions.). The good will be weighed against the bad, and the decision whether you live for an eternity in joy or pain will be given. To me, this Judgment Day sounds like a huge trial, where all of us are lined up and told of our doom or emancipation. To be honest, envisioning a whole horde of people doesn't make sense to me, determining all of our fates at once. Maybe there is a single file line where we wait for our individual turn, much like a lunch line at school where we wait to see if we get mock chicken legs or the real deal. But what do I know, except what's been written about it in the Bible, of course.

I do have an open mind when I hear about people who claim to have died and have been brought back to life to share stories of having their whole life shown to them, as if to review what they had done during their existence on Earth. Then instructions are sometimes given to the person being reviewed on things they should fix in their character, and they are then sent on their way back for more time here in this life. In a sense, this is judgment being given on a person, and apparently second chances are being given, too. I have also heard stories where the person being reviewed often gets to feel the effects of their negative actions on others, which sounds a lot like some form of punishment.

These stories of near death experiences are a little off the beaten path of traditional beliefs, but I sometimes find it hard to dismiss what people believe to have happened to them. That's an especially difficult task when similar reports come in from around the globe, making it less likely that these are all just coincidental occurrences. I'm not saying this is written in stone, but it shows there are many things to look at in faith searching. If all things are considered, it makes it hard to judge a person for getting a little confused in their quest for truth. There are tons of faiths to believe in out there, so who on Earth can say a person is wrong for their beliefs? Unfortunately, people still do.

Back to my thoughts on this Judgment Day thing: I wonder if we have a say in our trial to speak on our behalf for our reasons in making the decisions we did. In thinking about our American justice system, the time of judgment is when your pleading is not heard, just the decision made on your fate. Prior to this phase, though, you get to try to prove your case and why you are not deserving of any punishment.

I doubt God would be less just than our justice system and would allow us to speak, wouldn't He? Well, it says so here, at least, that when the day comes, we get to speak up for ourselves:

Romans: 14:12 "So then every one of us shall give account of himself to God."

–KJV

Let's take it a little bit further. Is God really placing judgment on us, or are our actions throughout our life speaking to Him for us where no words are needed? If you are condemned to an eternity of being far away from God, which would be torture in itself in my opinion, did He send you there?

With all that I have seen and remember in regard to God and now my visits with Jesus, I think there's a strong element we are missing — God is good!

I was taught so much about an angry God, to fear Him and His Power. But what is to fear if you are right with God and truly know it in your heart?

Trial day: So you are standing before God, and you personally know all that you have done in this life and what the consequences are. God looks at you and sees all of you, inside and outside, and knows your essence. If your heart exudes your true intentions throughout your life, although your actions got you into trouble at times, God will know it. If you took pleasure in wrong doings and made up for them wholeheartedly, God will know it. If you went out of your way to cause problems and did not care about what you had done, God will know that, too.

Not to compare God to a dog, but for crying out loud, if a dog can sniff that you have fear, don't you think God can tell that — and more? If God senses that you took pride in your wrongdoings and you emit that negativity, is He really calling judgment on you? God is good, and if you are not, you have nothing to do with Him. God is just returning the loyal subjects of evil back to whom they belong.

Now don't take this the wrong way, but it's acknowledged that it's necessary in most public places to divide the men's restroom from the women's restroom. Why this is done is up for debate, but I sure do feel more comfortable about this general rule. Personally, I don't want hundreds of men possibly aiming wrong on the seats of the lady's room, and in Heaven, the inconveniences could only mount higher with the opposite crowd there, too.

Men belong in their own restroom, to aim as they please, just as evildoers (Thanks, President Bush for making that word famous.) deserve to be returned to the one they listen to most. Of course, the same magnitude between these two, men and evil, are truly not to be compared (although some women would ask me to speak for myself and let the comparison remain as it is, but I'll be nice ☺).

Sigh . . . being turned away from God would be such a permanent death.

You know, I hear almost every day about a life cut too short, or a life lost at any age, and it hurts me. Death feels so wrong, so unfair, so unwanted, and yet it is so much a part of life. How could something so wrong and seemingly so dark truly belong to us?

Personally, I don't get it.

I don't know about you, but when I think about death and my loved ones who have passed, it doesn't feel like it was meant to be that way. It feels as if death is some kind of cruel joke being played on all of us by some joker in disguise. We fear the day that death happens to us, like some dark force creeping up to steal what is most precious to us.

I wonder what would happen if we all refused death. Would it then cease to exist? I suppose, right now that cannot happen in the physical world, but at least our souls can never die if we seek out God and Jesus for who They are.

Back to my other point. Why does darkness surround death, and why is anything dark associated with evil? Do you see where I'm going with this, or is my rambling that far off?

We are surrounded by darkness because of a decision that was made to allow darkness to be a part of our lives. A distinct decision was made a long time ago that somehow involved all of us. I just made use of my handy Bible program and thought I would start throwing in some more quotes here and there, so bear with me:

Genesis:

2:16. "And the Lord God commanded the man, saying, Of every tree of the garden thou mayest freely eat:"

2:17. "But of the tree of the knowledge of good and evil, thou shalt not eat of it: for in the day that thou eatest thereof thou shalt surely die."

3:5. "For God doth know that in the day ye eat thereof, then your eyes shall be opened, and ye shall be as gods, knowing good and evil."

And after man ate from the tree of the knowledge of good and evil:

3:22. "And the Lord God said, Behold, the man is become as one of us, to know good and evil: and now, lest he put forth his hand, and take also of the tree of life, and eat, and live for ever:"

–KJV

In a nutshell, the first man and woman God created didn't listen and ate from the tree of knowledge of good and evil, after being tempted by a serpent to do so. God found out, cursed women to suffer in childbirth (among other things), cursed the serpent to move only on his belly, and caused men to know of death. That is, there would be death unless we sought out God in some fashion to be given back eternal life.

Now, I wasn't there when this all took place and neither were you. But, somehow, because we all came from one woman all the way down the line, we all have the tree of knowledge fruit in us.

How would that make sense? I would guess it to be much like a woman who takes drugs while pregnant. When the woman's child is born, it is born with the drug in its system and the child is addicted to whatever the mom was taking. It takes time, but eventually the child gets the toxin out of its system, though the side effects can remain. With the right therapy, and working around the impairment of the child, the child can sometimes lead a healthy life.

I don't see why the same can't be for any of us then. Yes, some bad juice got into our system when the fruit of evil was ingested. Now we have had to search for this "tree of life" ever since, and obviously it can be found, since it was mentioned to be possible.

What a wonderful way to end a not-so-positive conversation: "You chose to get lost in the tunnels of darkness, but if you remember to reach up, you will find a light so that you can find your way out of them."

I can see why it is so tempting to find this gift of everlasting life. Not only is it a reward but also something that was once rightfully ours. We did have the ability to live forever in some God-given form! We had it once, so why not be able to take it back and show that we are responsible enough to maintain the privilege? Perhaps if enough of us prove to be worthy, we might pave the way for more of us to come.

These first two humans paved the way for evil to come into our lives, to end in death. So it would only seem plausible that the opposite could be done, as well. As I understand it, Jesus did just that by putting a marker on the road to point out the direction for us to take.

I know some people like to pick the Bible apart to see what fits into their belief system. But if you look at the whole text of the Bible, what is really so bad about it that anyone would have to fully shun parts of it? If you believe that two people decided that the knowledge of death would be with us, then why not the knowledge of everlasting life through the sacrifice of a man named Jesus? Is either story really any more seemingly farfetched than the other (I'm addressing those who might have a difference of beliefs with this statement here, as well.)? Jesus didn't do anything wrong; He woke people up to the reality of everlasting life.

I also believe He was a trendsetter of sorts in showing that there was a less structured way to faith, although, we only partially listened to that notion. In His life, He spoke about the confines of a lot of things people had in life that didn't need to exist. Being that men are vain and full of ego, no one liked the fact that anyone would dare claim to get their knowledge directly from God; but, since He is God's Son, He did dare. The people of that time could actually see Jesus and see a man before them who was actually within reach, while God was seemingly out of reach.

If something is too easy, it always seems that some men will turn it away as being false. Jesus was there, looking the men of that time in the eyes and performing undeniable miracles before thousands of people. To look away from Him and all that He was took some pretty hefty cans of ego to block Him out of sight!

Whether Jesus appeared to be a threat to the Roman Empire, which ruled the Jews in His time, or He bothered some high and mighty folks who liked the attention to be on them only, therein lies a controversy of who killed Him and why. Pointing a finger at anyone in particular doesn't help, especially since Jesus agreed to die for what He represented, way before anyone knew of His necessary sacrifice. All I know is, Jesus aimed to bring more focus to God, and He did a darn good job of it and saved our souls in the end.

I personally figure that enough suffering had come in the form of ignorance on how to find the "tree of life" that Jesus came to spell it out to people and made the necessary sacrifice with His own life. I don't think anyone of sound mind today can see what He did that was so wrong that He deserved to die as He did. He just opened up a lot of eyes to see how everlasting life could be achieved, and enough people apparently got the point to carry that message on. So again I ask, what was so bad about His message and actions, really?

~Tidbit: It surprises me that some people today don't even realize that the folks who carried on Jesus' message were, in fact, Jewish people. Some chose to follow His message, and some did not, just as people do today. So remember that the next time someone makes a comment that all Jewish people carry the blood of their ancestors, making them all responsible for His death, even

today. Some of their blood might be of the very line of Jewish disciples who helped get the word of Jesus directly to our ears.

Belief in Jesus started with His own people; there's no room for blaming any single person alive at present. If anything, we are all guilty that there had to be such a large sacrifice because of our wrongdoings.~

Why would any single person, ruler, religion, or community pooh-pooh the words which were spoken by Jesus, when He spoke only of positive things? I'm happy to say, in poor English for such a poor way of thinking, "I dunno!"

If your father hates the neighbors and insists you not speak to them, you might listen. When the men in power during Jesus' time felt threatened with Jesus, they aimed to instill in others that He was nothing more than a lunatic. It's hard to believe that some people actually listened to that and passed on that tradition of hate. But apparently it was already a tad too late to dismiss the thousands of people who saw for themselves the miracles which Jesus performed.

Do you really think that people would still be following the belief of Jesus, being who He said He was, without many people witnessing what He did in His life? It is a commonsense question that I think we all need to ask ourselves, because we know how the human condition is — we have to see it to believe it.

I'm saying, thousands witnessed Jesus speaking like no other, healing like no one before, bringing life to the dead, and He even rose from the dead. How can this be possible if He indeed was just a man who had lost His mind?

The only explanation for these miracles is that He was indeed who He and others said He was — The Son of God.

"What a cocky claim! How egotistical! What a big head he must have had!" So many have said these things, and many more will. Actions speak louder than words, though. Jesus' actions are still speaking across centuries, so it's pretty clear that there is more proof than any degrading words out there.

118

John:

14:6 "Jesus saith unto him, I am the way, the truth, and the life: no man cometh unto the Father, but by me."

14:7 "If ye had known me, ye should have known my Father also: and from henceforth ye know him, and have seen him."

14:11 "Believe me that I am in the Father, and the Father in me: or else believe me for the very works' sake." –KJV

He came to talk about, and for, His Father — God. By Jesus' miracles, they were to show what He spoke was the truth.

Does it really hurt us to know that Jesus is who He says He is? Some people I have met act as if it burns their ears to hear what they call rubbish. Still, I listen to their beliefs all the time, and it would be ignorant of me not to be able to stand to hear what they believe is the truth.

Everlasting life was proven and made achievable by Jesus' resurrection back to life. It can be reached by us all in the afterlife now, thanks to Him. You just have to accept this and not doubt that we are essentially good because we came from God. If God is good, then you originally came from good, which makes it possible to always go back to it. All you have to do is be true to who you are and reach for God for all of the right reasons. You owe it to yourself and to God to reclaim your humanity of life which was once lost from a poor decision made so long ago in the Garden of Eden.

No one makes decisions for you in what you do in your life, so don't let it be done in your afterlife, either. Make up your own mind whether your heart should listen to the stories of a Son named Jesus, who came to show people the way to eternal life. I know that it will not hurt you to know about Him, but it will hurt you not to know.

CHAPTER

13

HELL . . . I SHOULD HAVE KNOWN!

Oh, Hell, here we go.

Before I was opened up to seeing and understanding other realities, I thought Hell was some made-up world of fantasy my pastor and parents had created. It was hard for me to envision that "Hell is a place where all bad little girls and boys go who don't listen to their parents and won't do what they are told." That's not exactly how it was first presented to me, but it sums it up enough on how I interpreted these little Hell discussions.

It was just wild for me to think that such a place existed where I would be sent to be tortured by eternal flames just because I didn't make my bed and pick up my clothes. For the record, these two items are still a challenge for me, but I think God and I are cool about these issues now.

I would think, *Who could be so bad that God would throw them into some imaginary pit of flames that is said to be here on Earth somewhere?* I would think about my friends at school and how I saw them cheat on their tests, but that didn't seem Hell deserving. Then I would imagine kids throwing rocks at squirrels in the park, and still Hell didn't seem ready for them, either. When I thought of my sister sitting on me and stealing my candy, it was only then that I hoped Hell was a reality that some would be met with.

Wow! I thought, as a candy-lacking kid, *Hell truly is deserving for some people.*

Later, being somewhat grownup, I really didn't think much of the notion that there really was a Hell. It just seemed like a threat made to keep people in line — that extra push to have a reason to be good. In fact, it seemed quite logical to me after meeting some of the buttheads (Wow, no spell check error on that word — buttheads do exist.) I met in college who needed some monitoring.

"Just, go to Hell, you– you piece of crap!" Is something I think I have heard all too often with some added obscenities.

I knew God existed and that He was nothing but good. So I figured He wouldn't have allowed anything even close to the likes of Hell to exist.

Pause for dramatic build . . . Boy, was I wrong!

Hell was hard to keep a handle on. I mean, with all of our technology today and so many centuries later, Hell is still considered to be below our feet? I think it's a strange idea, but somehow this notion has lasted through time for a reason.

Well, I really got a chance to let the notion of Hell sink into my reality some time in 1998. This is when I had a tremendous waking dream that continues to move me until this day. I did the whole "getting ready and going to bed" routine, only to wake up and find myself as a resident of Hell.

Okay, I hope you are all done rolling your eyes to focus back to the page so I can continue.

Done?

Yes, I was there somehow, or it was a darn close virtual reality rendition. Don't ask me how, but I had apparently slipped into a person who had truly taken up residency in Hell. I knew that I had this person to move around in so that the "keepers" couldn't see who I really was, but other trapped souls could still see me for who I was. I remember walking very cautiously and looking over the horrible holding places of souls. I could even sense how some of these souls felt about their painful situation.

There were many dark tunnels, with iron bars and smelly, muddy rooms. People looked dazed, hopeless, and confused, as they crowded senselessly into rooms and corridors. Fear and nothingness seemed to be their essence, and there was no sense of purpose anywhere.

There were creatures that seemed enslaved to their own positions and wants, who wandered among the people as if to keep a close eye on them. Nothing seemed rushed, and I didn't see any fire-filled pits where people were being tortured, either. I only saw people in large groups, lingering as if they were waiting for something to happen. Yet, no feeling of anxiousness came from them, only heavy sorrow with lost tendencies sloughed off from them like chunks of dead skin.

When the creature keepers weren't looking, I approached the sad souls and told them, "Get ready; your chance to leave is coming soon."

The souls all knew what I was speaking of and nodded their heads in understanding, not wanting to draw attention to us talking. Their second chance at life was soon to be upon them, and it was something naturally understood by myself and the souls. It was a liberating feeling and yet somber when I realized what those souls would have to endure until that time came for them to leave.

I thought this waking dream was a pretty odd one, even for me. But I was quite happy when I found something that made me realize this experience wasn't to be taken lightly. This Bible program is fun with gathering quotes; look at what I found this time:

Revelations:

20:13 "And the sea gave up the dead which were in it; and death and hell delivered up the dead which were in them: and they were judged every man according to their works."

20:14 "And death and hell were cast into the lake of fire. This is the second death."

20:15 "And whosoever was not found written in the book of life was cast into the lake of fire."

–KJV

Everyone else seems to take a crack at interpreting the Bible; well this is my take since I had this Hell experience: It sounds like another chance to get a free ticket out of Hell, if a dead soul's judgment goes well.

This is a quote I didn't even know existed prior to my vision of Hell, so only more recently had I discovered any notion of this vision having any truth to be found in the Bible. I understand that people are being fooled all the time to serve darkness, and this often happens without them knowing they are doing so, as with some of these Hell dwellers. If that's the case, I think it's safe to assume they didn't take much joy in doing something they weren't even aware they were doing. That's a huge difference from someone knowing what they are doing that's causing harm and them taking pride in the pain they have caused.

If there is that difference in people who have been tricked into Hellish traps but have decent hearts, why wouldn't they get a chance to get out?

It was a huge surprise on my part to witness there being a second chance at all. A year prior to this revelation, a spiritual being spoke to me about there being a second chance for Hell residents. I hardly took the discussion seriously, since I hadn't even concluded there was a Hell to begin with.

Upon my leaving this Hell place and waking up in my bed the next morning with the memory fresh in my mind, only one element truly puzzled me; I had seen someone in the crowd who I knew to be not physically dead yet, but, nonetheless, she was a part of the inhabitants of Hell. In realizing this, I almost started to doubt what I remembered in visiting Hell.

As real as my experience was to me, it made no sense why living people were a part of this physical place. I found a way to keep the memory in my heart and mind as being a real experience, but that element of doubt crept in at times because of who I saw there.

It later dawned on me that if I could pay visits to the place I was more associated with (Heaven or what I often called the Crystal City), then why couldn't negative folks visit the place they were associated with (Hell)? It finally made sense to me.

Soon, I got justification for my thoughts on the Hell visits by other folks when random people began telling me about their Hell dreams. I often feel as if I have a sign on me somewhere which makes people feel comfortable to talk to me about their strange experiences, since it happens way too often, even when they don't know of my odd interest in these subjects.

One of the first Hell dreams I heard of was from a man I met while working at my grocery store job. He told me that one night he went to bed as usual and woke up in a small cage and was crammed in with a lot of other people. He cowered naked in this cage, fearing that the keeper would return. He said the smell of sulfur burned his nostrils. When he awoke the next day at home, he felt thankful that he lived another day to right his wrongs so he wouldn't return to that place.

It seems he might not have been quick enough to change his ways, however, since he had yet another visit to this place of horror. The last experience convinced him that he was not just dreaming of this place but that someday it would be his final destination. He then quickly turned his life around, got married, and became a leader in his church.

This man's mentioning of small cages in Hell soon became the norm that I would hear about from people who dreamt of Hell. The foul smell of sulfur was also a common element associated with this place. Another way of describing the smell, as one child I met told me, "It smelled like rotten eggs."

If I hadn't seen and experienced these very things myself, what these people were telling me would seem like a fantasy gone wrong. Knock on wood, sit on the cushion of your couch, feel the sun shining on your skin — this is the world I'm used to living in. What's this talk about some stinky place with cages and keepers with a knack for torturing people?

I know where people are in their thinking on this topic, because I was one of them. I sometimes wonder what's worse, being in the "know" or not knowing? I'm sometimes envious of people who are blind to anything on these topics. It just seems like it'd be so much easier to have only one life to worry about without including the afterlife segment, too.

Once I knew the reality of Hell, I couldn't help but worry about everyone around me, and if they were truly aware of it, too. But I didn't want to rain on anyone's parade with bad news, because once it really hits home, a person will feel the real threat that's present.

I know that when I would hear about people dying, under what circumstances, and how their loved ones who were left behind felt, a lot of things would enter my mind about the newly departed. I couldn't help but wonder if they were met with darkness on their passing, or if light had shown them the way home.

People mourn the loss of their loved ones, and I do as well, but my concern eventually gravitates toward the status of that departed person's soul. The odds are not good that peace is found by our deceased, and knowing this Hell-place firsthand, it doesn't help console me. So I suppose if I look at things in full view, raining on someone's short lifespan here to let them know about their Hell potential isn't such a bad thing after all.

Consider this your "Hell-o wakeup call," then. No one can pin me down for not sharing this information. As I've said before and will say again, "With knowledge comes responsibility."

Now you know it, and now you own up to it. It's not as if this is anything new that you haven't heard before, Hell has been explained to many of us — I would imagine. I just don't think people realize that once you have knowledge of it that it's considered a warning and that you can take heed — or not. Nice thought to have, isn't it?

After all that I had dealings with, I thought I had enough "in-your-face" Hell sputterings, but apparently, Jesus didn't think so. In April of 2000, Jesus thought it was a good idea to drop in on me again. I was at yet another conference, talking and mingling with other like-minded folks. I had met a University professor who was also a certified hypnotist at the same conference a few years back, and this year I asked him if he would try to regress me just to see if I had any random memories of any extraordinary or spiritual events in my life.

The hypnotist told me that he never guides a person to find anything in particular but instead lets them wander on their own to search out what they would like. So down the road to hypnosis I went, a road that had never worked for me in my search for knowledge, but I still tried to find the right person who could put me into a true hypnotic state anyhow.

A previous attempt with a hypnotist, who was also a friend, almost worked. But this current hypnotist was the first to get me into a truly relaxed state. I was able to envision all that he asked of me, even to the point of walking in a garden to find my own answers to questions I had about random memories.

With all I had experienced in my past, and how they were sketchy at times, I figured there had to be more to recall.

Once again, memories were not what surfaced in this attempt, either. I stepped into a garden of my choice that I was instructed to envision, and I began to describe to the hypnotist what I saw:

"Blue eyes," I said softly.

"Blue eyes?" The hypnotist repeated with a question.

"Yes . . . Him." Is all I could whisper out, while being shaken with awe.

Jesus had stepped into view, and He was so close to my face I could hardly speak. Blue eyes suddenly lit up within inches of my face, and His Presence flowed into me. Almost as if a light were being held behind a sky-blue screen, Jesus' eyes lit up my thoughts.

I wondered why I had never noticed His eye color before, then I somehow realized that the color I was seeing wasn't as they were here on Earth. They were unlike any eyes I had ever seen before. The closest comparison I can make as to how they appeared is to some characters in an awesome science fiction movie I have seen on several occasions called Dune. (See, having a thing for science fiction movies pays off.)

Without a word, Jesus led me toward the center of this garden, with a welcoming smile beaming from His soul. A long robe extended the full length of His body, and it appeared to be mostly white in color. I feel that I was peering into His face, but His eyes were so endearing that I did not want to pull away from them to take in much else about His face. Still, from my peripheral vision, I could see His long hair that seemed to rest lightly on His shoulders.

This meeting felt like a happy reunion of sorts, like friends gathering to share thoughts about their lives. Emotions were exchanged instead of words, where comfort and love was emitted from Him. He felt more casual and at ease than I had sensed in my meeting with Him just a month prior. It almost felt as if He could relax in knowing that He had gotten across to me the messages He wanted spoken. Then, as if matters were to be taken to another level, He wanted to show me what I was working toward.

I'm assuming that in this envisioned garden of mine, I had walked down a flight of stairs to relaxation. When I entered this garden of green grass and trees, it was surrounded by hillsides that were cut to fit this garden in their center. It was as if I had walked down into the valley of this place, to find a perfectly cut out and well-groomed garden grove. Upon reflecting on what this place looked like, I believe it looked more like a small park. Still, somehow the word "garden" always seems to pop into my mind first whenever I speak of this visit.

While Jesus and I stood in the center of this garden, directly in front of us was a short path that led up to the cut-off side of one of these hills. I hadn't noticed it before, until Jesus brought forth the proposal of wanting to show me something. He held up one of His hands as if to present the path for me to follow.

I felt as if I floated along the short route until it ended at the foot of the hill. It was there I saw a wooden door at the base of the hill, yet another element I didn't initially notice. Jesus was present. I supposed that I was so focused on Him that I hadn't fully taken in my surroundings to notice everything.

Jesus touched the door and it opened immediately. I peered inside to see a dark tunnel surrounded by a wall of mud and protruding roots of the vegetation growing on the hill. I could smell the dank scent of moisture coming from the mud in the tunnel, and I wondered where we were going that Jesus felt was so important for me to see.

He led me inside, and the tunnel quickly grew dark to where I couldn't see in front of me. I didn't want to fully lose sight of where Jesus was, so I picked up my pace and clung close behind Him. I could feel His robe gently brushing against me in the dark, and I almost wanted to grab hold of His robe for security. His Presence was so strong, however, that I didn't feel it truly necessary for me to reach for Him — He was already there for me.

The tunnel was probably not as long as it seemed. It also was not truly tall enough for me to stand in without ducking slightly to avoid the roots hanging down in my face. Still, at times, the rough mud edges of the tunnel brushed my head slightly, causing me to bend down even more.

Soon, a second door became apparent in the darkness in front of Jesus, as He and I huddled slightly on the muddied path. He then turned to me, and I felt Him ask with His heart, "Are you ready?"

The door opened, and Jesus stood in the tunnel and partially hunkered down, so I could easily peer over His shoulder. To my shock, I saw a narrow, rock-carved bridge that had free-fall canyons on both sides. On the opposite end from where we stood, the bridge widened slightly to a platform, just before an iron gate. This gate was attached to a stone wall that seemed to extend forever in each direction. Deep drop-offs ran along the side of the wall, which would make leaving this place a physical impossibility.

Through the gate bars, I could see at least one creature pacing back and forth. I wish there is some way to describe what it looked like, only to say it was dark gray, hunched, and with long arms. It appeared to look our way when Jesus opened the door and responded by pacing rapidly back and forth.

As I looked over Jesus' shoulder and took in all there was to see, I understood what He was saying to me. *He was taking me on a tour of Hell!*

I looked into Jesus' eyes and saw the invitation waiting there for me to accept. I looked back over the bridge and reflected on what I had already endured in seeing this place in my waking-dream and feeling the souls of those lost there. The feeling was too overwhelming for me to think I would have to see this place again just to be sure I had gotten the message.

My thoughts went back to Jesus, who was still partially crouched in front of me so that I could see past Him. I gazed into His eyes, and I knew the choice was mine to accept, or not. So I said to Him, "No. I remember this place. You don't need to show me again."

129

I felt Jesus smile in acknowledgment as He slowly closed the door to Hell in front of us. We turned around in the tunnel, facing the light that led back to the garden. We passed so quickly through the tunnel that it seemed we were almost immediately out of the darkness and back into the light.

I remember standing just outside the tunnel with the door closed, and His blue eyes were very close to mine. Those eyes smiled at me with what felt like a million hugs coming from Jesus, and then the vision began to fade.

I left the garden and soon drifted back into this reality. Upon returning, I could feel I was back in my body and aware of my surroundings. There was something else that I felt as I lay there — I had opened up to myself. Some would call it your "higher self", but I just call it the "real me who knows what happened before I landed my astral butt here." When I relate this story to people about declining the invitation from Jesus to take a tour of Hell, they can hardly believe that I did such a thing. I can see their point on this, since it was a pretty huge deal to even have that chance.

After having seen so many things regarding the Hell topic and having heard all of the testimonies from people, I had a pretty clear understanding of it. The topic didn't need to be driven home any more in me to understand the full package of Hell. Jesus also could tell I had gotten the full idea, or I'm certain He would floated the message that there was something more that I didn't understand.

When Jesus led me along that path toward the pits of Hell, I knew His message was to let me know what I was working for. That goal entails helping people become aware of this place so they can avoid it and helping those who have already fallen victim there.

I remembered those things quite well; besides. they were pretty hard lessons to forget. A solo trip to Hell, Hell-dweller's eyes on you, and stories of Hell pouring your way from strangers can really open your eyes to being convinced.

Why Jesus chose to pop up as He did, I cannot say. However, I do know it's not a coincidence that He drops by when I am in a relaxed state, such as while sleeping and attempting regression. I know I am capable of focusing on more otherworldly things when my body isn't fully aware of where it is and what it's doing. There are millions of sensory-input nuggets communicating with my body and its environment all the time, so it's no wonder that I need to numb myself from this reality before I can see the underlying reality.

I can just imagine, with so many things going on with me, that it would be hard to get a message across in my normal state: My arms are resting on the chair, my stomach is digesting — oh, hold on, there's nothing in there — I'm hungry, swallow, blink, move hair out of eyes, dilate pupils, sniff, scratch, wonder what's on TV, and where's the bathroom?

I'm sure that my thoughts are a huge distraction and even more so when I think of my bodily functions going on, too. So it really doesn't surprise me that my visits come only when I can pull myself away from at least some of these distractions. I guess to experience things of a spiritual nature, I have to be more in the spirit of things. This last visit from Jesus, I felt, was a more personal visit than anything, to make sure that my goals were clear. I don't know of any grand message I can relay to anyone about this besides the obvious — that Hell exists — except to say that Jesus is something else!

Well, I guess there is one small detail I can relate about this visit, and Hell, which might hit a chord with some folks. The fact that there were actually gates to Hell shocked me! I have heard that term about opening the gates to Hell, and there they were in front of me. Hmmm... but aside from that fact, Jesus was there to help me out in my purposes.

I feel very fortunate that I received special insights to help me on my journey, yet I can wish until I am blue in the face that I see Jesus right now and have Him reveal some great revelation

131

to me again. Most likely it won't happen — wait, hold on — no, it's not happening.

I've learned that patience is the key with anything related to spiritual matters. The true realization of Hell is a mouthful to swallow whole. Taking bits and pieces and chewing it up nicely seemed to prevent it from getting lodged in my throat.

Ask any speech therapist who instructs others on how to digest best: "Don't take in a lot of air, chew thoroughly, and try not to talk when your mouth is full." People tend to eat too quickly and they choke and spit up things that are good for them, so nutrients never reach their target.

Yeah, yeah, another weird analogy. But you know what? I came across an interesting comment that Jesus made to one of His disciples in the Book of Matthew. To many of you, this is old news, but for me everything hits a little deeper now since my encounters with Him.

In this book it was asked why Jesus spoke in parables, or short little tales. Jesus replied that He did that so people could fully relate to what He was talking about by comparing His message to everyday instances. He went on to say that not everyone would be able to grasp His messages if they were directly spoken of. I guess you can say I am borrowing from Him on how to get points across in this book. I doubt that He has patented His teaching technique, so I think I'm safe in not needing a signed release from Him.

With that said, you can be sure there will be more of my odd analogies to come.

MINI-CHAPTER

14

EVIL REVELATIONS

Ya know, I'm sitting here thinking on how I can make my point about a few things without dedicating a whole, big chapter to them. Then it dawns on me, "Hey, I'm writing this book! I haven't followed any rules yet, so why start now? Thus, 'twas born "Mini-Chapters!" So here they begin:

Hell was indeed hard to ingest, but I wanted to mention some things about Hell on Earth. Not literally, I should say, until the Bible Chapter of Revelations comes to light. I'm speaking more of the evil that can be seen in this world. Jesus gave me some tidbits to chat about, so I'm going to be just a little preachy here while I can (As if I haven't already — right — so it happened more than I expected.).

When I have told people about Jesus, a lot of them have asked me if I asked Him why this or that happens to us. It always seems to come up that people feel God or Jesus has turned Their backs on us to allow horrible things to exist the way they do here on Earth. It's always, "Why do people starve to death? Why is there so much hate in the world? Why doesn't God strike down more men with lightning bolts?"

133

For the record, I didn't get to ask Jesus all of these questions, either. But I feel it's not a stretch that we all need to own up to some of the responsibility for what goes on here. There's always a cause and effect: I hit a ball and the ball flies through the air (If it's not a ground ball.). If a person entertains bad thoughts, bad things can come of it, which will affect assorted things down the line. There's a difference between bad thoughts coming into your mind and you rejecting them, and them coming in and you actually thinking them over as a possibility.

Everyone gets these stray thoughts that we know we shouldn't act on but would love to — at times, anyway. I bet there are a ton of sweet little grandmas out there with thoughts of punching someone in the nose, although they don't actually do it. The more we practice self-control over thoughts of actions like these, the stronger we get to fight off negative thoughts. To slip sometimes, though, is not necessarily a free ticket to Hell, as far as I understand. If that were true, the Earth might as well open wide and take a big gulp — we'd all go down with it!

We currently have chance after chance to miss out on spending eternity in pain while residing in Hell. Speaking of which, another question I get sent my way is, "What's the purpose of people suffering for an eternity, anyway?" It seems logical to me, as well, that not too many people really have done that many horrible things to keep on being tortured forever.

I have learned a lot about this topic from all kinds of sources, including stories people have revealed to me about their encounters with dark creatures. Negative forces love to feed on the fear we give them. Just as the sun shining down on our skin gives us needed nutrients and energy to get through the day, these negative forces feed off of the darkness, pain, and fear. It might seem invisible to us to fully understand that kind of feeding process, much like our body feeding off the sun, but that doesn't mean it doesn't happen.

It would seem hard to believe that such things exist, yet we watch the news and hear about monsters all the time. There are rapes, murders, and child molestation stories constantly before our eyes. For these things to keep happening, there must be some sort of pleasure being had in watching another person suffer. In a sense, the habitual offenders of these and other crimes are feeding on the pain they are causing others.

It has been scientifically noted that for some people there's an adrenaline rush caused by performing criminal acts, which can be quite addictive for the habitual offender. This is not even mentioning the feeling of invulnerability and superiority the offender feels while committing their crimes. So to think that there are creatures out there that take pleasure in torturing people — well, I don't think it's much of a stretch at all that this is being done in a place we tend to call Hell.

Hopefully, this will get people to think twice before they dismiss the possibility of there being a destined place for the similar negativity we see on Earth, just in a more concentrated form.

Even our own society has dedicated a place for offenders of our made-up rules. Yep, we call our little form of justice the penitentiary, prison, lockup, or the "Big House". If we have allowed such a place to exist in our culture in order to keep structure in our society, perhaps we got that idea from somewhere else. I don't think I have to spell it out, but thinking of the holding place called Hell just might give you a clue.

Is this evil being fought with evil? Sheesh! That's a hard one to answer. Even to say it's a necessary evil isn't good to suggest. I guess it's best to say that it's the only way our society knows how to deal with people who are out of line with our community. Of course, there are those who are wrongly accused and suffering for no good reason, too. Well, now, that sounds familiar for some of those folks in that Hell place. The only difference is, we just don't make any promises to revisit the circumstances as it's said in the Bible in the verse I shared earlier (Romans 14:12).

Now, to apply the same question as Hell being a necessary evil, dang it, I don't know why I even try to take on such hard questions! Well, perhaps it's the solution for now. From what I hear, things are supposed to be changing at some point.

All I know is that evil exists, plain and simple, and you only have to look around to see it. It is there, but no one should feel that all is hopeless because it has existed for so long in all of the worst places. Remembering that evil won't prevail in the end should really be a soothing remedy for all that ails our minds. Like budding leaves in the spring after a Wisconsin winter's thaw, Jesus will give new life to the world we see now.

Change is on its way.

15

WHAT IS HE LIKE, AND WHAT SHOULD WE BE LIKE?

Whenever I reflect on all I felt coming from Jesus, I wish I could just peel open my soul for others to feel what I did. This place called Earth can be seen as such a beautiful place, but to many of us it doesn't look so great. We go to places like the Gulf of Mexico and see all of the beauty that surrounds the area, but how does it look to the many residents who live in poverty there in Mexico? I would imagine that for some it's hard to fully appreciate your surroundings if you are in a terrible bind.

This leaves me to wonder if all people perceive beauty or love in the same manner. I wonder what it takes for a person to overcome their situation to indeed reach their full potential in experiencing and encouraging others to look beyond their physical situation and more toward the light.

Jesus lived a life of great joy, but He saw great pain, too. Imagine being persecuted for talking about your personal beliefs in a time when that was punishable by death. I realize that it still happens today in some places; what a horrible reality that must be. With that kind of situation at hand, it takes a special person to rise above it and still seek to open people's minds to other possibilities.

That was Jesus then, and the Jesus now doesn't seem to be much changed, aside from being able to come and go as He wishes.

He has a sense of humor, a deep and profound one at that. Love is laughter, and He seems to find great joy in revealing this side of Him. I don't know if my love for toilet humor (meaning: as in everything that relates to an actual toilet, as in comical toilet scenes from movies) quite fits the same bill. But, hey, I find a lot of joy in it (I just can't speak for everyone else on this subject.).

Jesus, on the other hand, has one of those contagious feelings of joy. Have you ever known someone who could laugh their thighs off, but you haven't a clue what is so funny and you join in the laughter anyway? That's the kind of joy you see and feel with Jesus, where you can't help but want to join in on that special something He has going on.

If Jesus is a reflection of His Father, I don't see anything to fear if you are aiming to be on His side of the good-versus-evil battle. I doubt many of us are eagerly waiting to join forces with darkness, and if you are, there's something truly wrong in your life.

I know there are some people out there who are thinking, *"I'll do whatever I want! Nobody cares about me anyway, so why should I?"*

This is especially true when it comes to teenagers who might perceive a lack of love and understanding in their life, which can accumulate into a breakdown on a lot of levels. Truth is, there *are* people who truly care in this world, and that Son named Jesus can be counted as one of them.

It can't always be helped that a person has met rotten people most of their lives, where they might feel there is no hope for peace. But if that person can keep faith that they can find some decent folks to surround them, love will come. Negativity made its presence known here long before any of us ever came along, and it will be here for a little while yet, so there's no need to add to it. Lashing out to hurt yourself or someone else, no matter how badly you might feel, solves nothing. What we can all do is to be a beacon of light that can be seen by others who are searching for a gleam of hope in this life. If a person is keen enough to recognize that the people around them are not positive, then that person is strong enough to see that they can start a change. Not all people can see that change needs to happen and can actually be made to happen.

Jesus is a good example of how one person can make a difference and stand out in a crowd for others to seek out help. Of course, He had that added Son of God trait that made Him sparkle quite a bit more than others, but He still serves as an example for everyone to follow. No, we can't be exactly as He was. If that were possible, there would have been no need for Him.

Obviously, then, it is not the case that we need to strive to be perfect. Failure will no doubt keep plaguing us, so doing our true best should suffice. We were given the choice to figure right from wrong for a reason. We know the difference! No one can tell me that they don't know that it's wrong to take a rock and hit someone with it. There are also those subtle instances where we know something is wrong to do, like when we know it's wrong to talk badly about someone. We have this gut feeling with which God equipped us, telling us if something is right or wrong.

We are, of course, bound to make mistakes, and Jesus seemed to acknowledge "mistake makers" and still invite them to be a part of His group of disciples. From what I understand, no one is a complete loss, according to Jesus. All people have the chance to rise above what they are doing, make a complete change in their lives, and become followers of God.

I have often wondered if people who have committed awful crimes in their lives had the same opportunities we did. In using my own brain noodle, I don't remember anyone saying, "All God's children can be saved — except for the rapists, murderers, thieves, vandals, liars, cheaters, abusers, prostitutes, drunk drivers, drug dealers, and addicts!" I realize none of these things were ever smiled upon and were often preached on and against in the Bible.

I just cannot imagine the man I met named Jesus would ever say, "Sorry you did these things, so you might as well give up in trying to make up for them."

Bible search program to the rescue again:

Ephesians:

2:8 All will be forgiven . . . even though not deserved by any of our actions

$$-KJV$$

Forgiveness is for everyone!

Being the victim, or even being related to the victim of a horrible crime, it might be hoped that the person who committed the criminal act will rot in Hell for what they have done. However, to see to it that the criminal does indeed meet God sooner than planned is not our place.

God will get to them in His own time, so don't worry about it. We should feel sorry that the criminal has such a long road ahead to get back in God's favor. We should also realize that God turns His back on no one who asks Him to enter their life. Priests and ministers still visit our prisons to spread the Word of God, to add to God's army, because there still are sparks of God's light in all people.

Being a serious criminal who enjoys his offenses is one thing, and living the life God gave us where we commit tons of mistakes is the rest of us. We do have to goof up sometimes in order to learn the right thing to do next time so we don't repeat ourselves. If we do repeat ourselves, well, then we are just human and it's okay. But it's not okay to keep on doing the same thing without remorse or feeling, "Oh, heck, God will forgive me anyway, so I'll just ask Him again, once I'm done doing the same rotten thing."

God ain't dumb, people! (Yeah, I said ain't.)

We do have to "live a little" and making mistakes along the way will inevitably happen. These mistakes can be big or small ones.

Some of us might steal things but return to pay for them, might laugh at our friend who fell down but help him up, yell to be heard only to apologize later, speed but learn to stay within the speed limit, fail in school but remain to graduate, have a baby while you're young but still pursue your dreams, be in trouble when you were young but teach your kids to do better!

Now I'm wondering if I'm forgetting something. I think I've got it all out about Jesus: He's a rich soul, full of joy, strong, happy, anxious to return, determined, concerned, and loving.

I think I plopped out how we humans are and should be, too: Faithful, full of mistakes; have fun, full of mistakes; live a little, full of mistakes; work hard, full of mistakes; loving, full of mistakes; forgiving, full of mistakes; never give up.

What's not clear?

16

THAT SOUL THING

Now to talk a little bit about our souls and — uh, some other stuff about them. If it dawns on you that you actually have a soul, then you need to feed it, meaning giving your soul what it needs in order to survive, to live long and prosper, to get the upper hand, to speak when spoken to, to straighten up and fly straight, and any other saying of value.

It just crossed my mind again how so many people still doubt the full existence of the soul. You can think of it as the driver of the car that you get around in now — the one called your body. It's the programmer behind your favorite game — called your life. It's the grease in your burger that helps it slide down your throat — called essential calories (for some of us, at least). The soul is who we really are, plain and simple. Jesus pointed the way to knowledge about the potential of our souls. He also showed us the way to correct and avoid the bad things which can corrupt our souls. He even showed us that if corruption occurs and corrections are needed and made, then they would be duly noted by God if done as instructed.

Unfortunately, not all of us have taken heed of His directions. Doing half-fast (meaning: quickly yet poorly done) tasks are a way of life these days. It seems that most of us hope to reap the benefits of our actions with the least amount of effort.

As a person who might be worried about doing enough to please God so they can have that eternal life gig, taking into full account of what's necessary to maintain our souls should be a priority. But falling down on our soul's face because of our slacking doesn't always mean we are doomed.

Think of it this way: Say you instructed your kids on how to wash the dishes properly with soap and water. You point out to them that they had to do this for themselves because it was out of the jurisdiction of their babysitter who is watching them for a few days. For all other needs, the babysitter will be there for them.

You make certain to warn your kids that if they don't listen closely on how to wash these dishes, there's a good chance that bacteria will creep into their system and make them ill. So you make it clear that they are responsible for this chore and to not steer toward any shortcuts, because there is no other way to accomplish their task except how you showed them.

You, the parent, now leave for your little weekend getaway with no worries that your kids won't do as they are told. The weekend passes, and upon your announced return you find your kids sick and rolling on the floor, holding their bellies in agony. You soon learn that they only partially listened to what you said about washing the dishes with soap and water. Only rinsing of the dishes took place, in hopes of fooling you into thinking they had done as they were told.

On the surface, the dishes looked clean enough, but their deceit is more than apparent with their present condition. Your children are remorseful now for not listening, and they plead with you to help them feel better. They promise to listen closer the next time and swear not to do only a rinse job on the dishes again.

As a loving parent, you cannot conceive of leaving your child in agony as a punishment for their disobeying. Little did your children know that you have already called for an appointment with a doctor where they'll be met with caregivers who will prescribe antibiotics to fight what ails them. You are just happy that you got to them before their illness took a turn for the worse.

Quite a long analogy, but one I felt necessary in getting a point across. Being imperfect human beings, even when it comes to matters of the soul, we often don't follow every rule given to us. But does that mean we are doomed and won't be helped after falling to the ground, holding our bellies?

This is sounding preachy, isn't it? But really, we need to think about this. Even being the flawed folks we are, we wouldn't leave our kids to suffer, and we have to realize that God wouldn't either.

All is not lost!

Just as you, the parent, will take your kids to a doctor for the right medicine, God will lead you to the right people to give you a chance at being well — spiritually speaking. There's always a way to bring your soul back to its full luster and health. It's hoped that we all learn our lessons when we are down so as to not go back to the stage we were at — but crap happens! Yet, it doesn't mean we can't try again until we get ourselves right.

I want to keep saying to people, "Don't you know you have a soul?" As long as it is a part of you, it can be flawed. God knows this. He knows that we are not perfect on any level. But what we *can* do is work at it and try not to do that "quick fix" on getting ourselves right, because it leaves room for bacteria of the spiritual realm to creep into us. Besides that, God will know that you tried to cut corners to look good to others — but it won't work on Him; corners don't exist which are able to block His View.

None of this "soul business" is about looking good; it's all about actually *being* good. This goodness comes from the inside and works its way toward the outside. There are no time limits on when you can make a change in yourself, but, as I've mentioned before, it helps not to wait until the last minute. If death comes to you before you allow God's thoughts to enter your life, you can be sure, that is not a good time.

Don't let anyone say to you in this life that you are worthless and can never change, to the point where you'll doubt yourself and fall for what others have told you. It's not up to them to decide your destiny, nor should you be out to prove to anyone that you *have* changed. Thumb your nose at them or do something to get them off your back — or just plain ignore them.

What you do to make things better with your soul is between you and God. People and the holes in their faces that flap out hunks of negativity at you should not be the ruling party in your life. Making the changes in our lives is what matters for us, and to God. As long as He can see what you are doing, there's no need to worry about having any other witnesses to the 'New You'.

This isn't a haircut I'm talking about. It goes a bit deeper than that. There is no one on this green Earth who can outright define who you are and where you'll end up. Each of us, as individuals, has the distinct choice at hand every day and every hour, even right down to the seconds. Making plans to change your life doesn't have to be a formal affair, where you pick the even days out of the month, or a holiday.

We really have some weird practices on this planet, don't we? I always hear about people starting diets, quitting smoking, or reducing nail biting at the beginning of the New Year, after the divorce, when they've moved, or after final exams. What's wrong with the moment you are wiping the sweat off your brow, bathing your dog, or driving in your car to work?

You don't want me to get started on my bit on being informal on the toilet again, do you? All right then, so what's your next excuse?

There aren't any, so be done with it. Begin, fall down, get back up again, slip, kneel, and back into a belly flop! At least make an honest effort to bring your soul to light, and I'm sure God will find a lot to smile about. ☺

17

DISTRACTIONS

Ever hear someone say something like, "Oh, don't give me that God crap! If you ask me, all you have to look forward to is what you see in front you today. In my case, it's a load of manure, so I suggest you grab a shovel and start spreading the same joy I'm feeling right about now!"

Sounds like this person has the appropriate job in front of them, since shoveling crap seems to be their specialty (I love that word crap.)!

Distractions can appear from anywhere, but it seems people have cornered the market in being key to blocking another's view to spirituality. There is always going to be someone with a varying opinion when it comes to matters of the soul. It can be especially difficult to talk about when someone like your parents or your best friend has a strong negative opinion on the subject.

There are a lot of people who are soft-spoken with less confidence in standing their ground on issues when they talk with other people. Politics, religion, and other people's weight are topics to avoid if you want to stay out of trouble. Yet many people can be out-talked and belittled by loud-mouthed "know-it-alls" while talking about almost anything.

It's something to keep in mind, though; blockheads who have a bigger mouth than you doesn't mean they are right.

This goes for anyone you know, and for a variety of instances, even outside of a typical conversation. Just to throw some examples out there on how wrong others can be, although you might feel or know differently:

Let's see, there's the police officer who won't listen to you and busts you for something your passenger shoved under your car seat. There can also be your parents, who teach you to hate other races in God's Name, because, after all, your race is smiled upon more than others. There can also be the priest who teaches unsuspecting gays in their church to hate themselves, while that priest molests children behind closed doors. I'm not bad-mouthing all priests, of course, but, hey, these things *do* happen. Let's be real.

All of these instances involved a bit of trust in the other person before varied forms of betrayal happened. People just seem to do and say things that help them feel better about themselves so they can cope better in the physical sense only. So in thinking of matters of what their actions do to their soul, or the condition of another's soul, I doubt if it even crosses their minds a lot of the time.

Those pesky little varmints of distractions are always with us.

Not only are our souls not regarded in a lot of instances, due to our own victimization and others, but other basic essentials in our lives can also distract us to where our soul doesn't always come to mind first.

The fact is, people, we need to eat! With even that single necessity, a lot of distractions can come into play. Try waking up early in the morning, aiming to meditate or pray, when all you can think about is your stomach that woke up with you.

Yet, to get food into your belly is no easy matter. First, you have to have a job, and that job helps you produce trade value that we like to call the "Almighty Dollar" in the United States. With that dollar, you have to gain transportation, and that can be anything from a bus, a bike, to a beat-up car so you can haul yourself to the grocery store. Once at the store, you get a shopping cart that squeaks and bangs to the beat of 80s music playing from the store ceiling speakers.

While there, you bump into someone you know but cannot stand to be near. A conversation ensues, and you try to escape by pushing your cart down the aisle, but your assailant follows. You finish shopping and reach the checkout line where you are the 10th person in line — with that blabbermouth still on your heels. After several price checks, mothers fanning through coupons, and high school kids counting out small change, you reach the cashier only to find that you left your checkbook at home!

Embarrassment and pain makes your head throb, as the biggest headache of your life singes your brain. Thoughts of shoplifting enter your mind as you wish for the cash to buy the aspirin you see within reach. Instead, you head for the door, trip off the curb, wait for your bus in the rain, reach home, plop on your couch, and mumble, "Life sucks!"

Oh, the inconvenience which life can bring, and to think, that was just one little task. No one said life would be easy, but there is some comfort in knowing that we all struggle in our own ways. Sure, there are some people who are loaded with all the cash and physical conveniences they could want. It all sounds good and sweet, right?

Not always. Just do a search online to look up some of the hottest stars of today, and of the past, and see what they have gotten themselves into. They have so much "stuff" to keep them entertained on the outside, but there are so many of them who are always trying to reflect the same on the inside by fooling themselves with drugs and alcohol! Then there are the young stars who get a ton of credit and attention and fall into miserable traps of eating disorders and other various problems.

It sounds ridiculous that a superstar should have self-destructive tendencies, yet it happens. Again, each person has his own struggles in life, in his own way. To wish you were someone else is not the key to positive thinking. Changing the way you live brings the positive spark your way as well as thinking positively.

While latching onto some memories and what Jesus has taught, it seems that simplifying our lives is huge in getting things in order with our souls and lives. I don't recall Jesus saying, "Collect as many material things as you can so you can take them to Heaven with you." He didn't serve as an example for men to live large and enjoy all of the spoils of a rich man.

Instead, Jesus wandered from place to place, speaking to anyone who would listen to the message of a better place that we can all attain. He didn't seem to place restrictions on His cause. He let people know that He was the Bridge to God for all to cross over, back to His Home in Heaven.

Yes, I know there are quotes all over the Bible which say, "Do this to get that — or else!" But when I look at the whole picture of what Jesus stood for, His sacrifice opened the gates for all people to go through — if they so choose.

Choosing the right way is of utmost importance, and it's not the easiest way, either. I like to think of challenges in life and spirit as being fun and full of adventure. If everything were too easy, where's the sense of accomplishment? Instead, look at your challenges as something to meet with vigor and faith.

I admit I have had my share of wishing that life just paid out already, because I was done with struggling. But I remember how good it felt when I saved and bought my first set of used furniture, bought a much deserved outfit, and got my first car after years of taking the bus. This is a list of only material things, but they were also comforts to me in my personal life.

The thrills I got by reaching certain milestones made me want to accomplish even more. They were priceless moments. Making everything count in life with meaning has always helped me. We can't all have what others have. Diversity keeps things interesting while we are here.

Avoiding the topic of those who outright suffer in life is not my style, though. When it comes to others suffering, while there are people near who are able to put out a helping hand to aid in their pain, there comes that magic word again — "responsibility".

You'd better believe that we are each responsible for ignoring some of the bigger distractions in this life. So, you might be a little late in getting to work because you saw a beggar and bought him something to eat or drink. You might be late for your favorite television program because your friend was down on her luck and needed someone to talk to. You might be late reaching your destination because you stopped on the highway to help someone whose car broke down.

I cannot help but think that some distractions are tests to see who we really are. Of course, we can't always stop our lives to take care of every needy soul we come across — or can we? Jesus appeared to take time for all who came His way, and if He is to be the example we all follow, we sure do have a lot of catching up to do.

In all honesty, none of us can compare to Him, what He did, and what He continues to do. If we all practiced doing as He did in even the smallest of capacities, there would be much less suffering. We would all pick up the loose ends in this society and take care of each other's needs when they appear.

If we all were on top of each other's pain, poverty wouldn't be an issue. Food would immediately be provided, and housing would be made available worldwide, regardless of politics. If someone were in need of medical care, they would be given the best treatment and medicines available. There would be no insurance checks to go through to determine if the bill would be paid in full, and being a caregiver at a hospital would then have its true meaning. Medicines would be provided without pharmaceutical companies limiting drugs that produce cures because there's less profit to be made with healthy people walking around. Harmful gossip about someone would be halted as soon as it began, since negative emotions would be realized as a real oppressor to positive thinking.

Oh, the dreams of having a worldwide conscience. It would almost be like Heaven on Earth, in a sense. But, alas, we are a species of people lacking in focus in this world of distractions and entertainment.

I fall into the same predicament of rationalizing why I shouldn't stop for every beggar on the street or pause to help every person with a problem, too. If only we all counted to three and fixed what was around us, I might actually be up to par in doing my part.

For now, I'll do what I can and hope other people will make the conscious decision to do what they can to help bring this dream to a reality.

Revelations:

21: 1 "And I saw a new heaven and a new earth: for the first heaven and the first earth were passed away; and there was no more sea."

21:2 "And I John saw the holy city, new Jerusalem, coming down from God out of heaven, prepared as a bride adorned for her husband."

–KJV

The above mentioned dream of John is one "dream" that I am certain most of us hope was no dream at all . . .

MINI-CHAPTER

18

FACELESS

Questions, questions, questions . . . one of the most popular
questions I hear regarding Jesus is why I could not see His face.
Simply put, I don't think what He looked like is what was important.
With the tendency that man has to create idols to focus our eyes
to, I am not surprised that Jesus didn't allow me to remember His
face. This doesn't mean He hasn't shown others what He looks
like. I have read of other encounters from people who claim to
have seen His features in some detail.

Appearances are an interesting topic, but the message of His
contact should be more of the focus. If you went to your mom
for advice, would you over analyze what she was wearing and
see if her fashion statement would help remedy what ails you? It
sounds ridiculous to even think about an odd factor as petty and
superficial as what your mom is wearing, right?

I described what I saw when Jesus approached me only
because it sure did stimulate my eyeballs with what I was
witnessing, although what happened on the inside of me was more
sensational than anything my eyes could ever interpret.

I must admit that after seeing Him that first time, I actually
did want to keep in mind that wonderful light which poured

from His soul and into mine. So I headed out to some Christian shops looking for a drawing of Jesus where light spiraled out from His heart. For me, it was more of a reminder of His Love than His image, which also kept in mind what experiencing Him did for me.

Ah, I just thought of that exhilarating feeling I got from Him again. Sheesh! I doubt I'll ever get over it . . .

Now, where was I? Facelessness, oh, wow, spell-check didn't even try to stop me from using that word. I wonder how often that comes up, where facelessness is an issue. Strange society, indeed.

When I personally thought about why I didn't get to actually see, or remember seeing, Jesus' face, another reason crept into my mind when I came across this quote:

Hebrews:

8:10 "For this is the covenant that I will make with the house of Israel after those days, saith the Lord; I will put my laws into their mind, and write them in their hearts: and I will be to them a God, and they shall be to me a people:"

8:11 "And they shall not teach every man his neighbor, and every man his brother, saying, Know the Lord: for all shall know me, from the least to the greatest."

–KJV

I wondered if this all went back to something I mentioned earlier about judgment not only being judgment. If you have little to do with God, then you are to leave His sight. Perhaps this can be related to people recognizing Jesus for who He is without being told, but, instead, knowing it from the inside. God says here that no one will have to be taught on knowing Him, because it's already in each and every one of us to know Him.

Tons of people have this attitude, where they don't believe something until they see it for themselves. It's not that they cannot see these things for themselves, but with that kind of attitude, they could be waiting for a lifetime to have their eyeballs enlightened to seeing what they want. All that time is then wasted when they could have been seeking and growing.

We are not to be catered to, for people to serve us and fill our bellies and minds with what we need. Some effort has to be put forward to get answers on our own, to show we are good candidates for some insight.

"Seeing to believe" is not a good philosophy to go by. Why not try that faith thing out and see if you can first believe and perhaps have your chance to see?

After His resurrection, Jesus came to His disciples and said: *John: 20:29*

"Jesus saith unto him, Thomas, because thou hast seen me, thou hast believed: blessed are they that have not seen, and yet have believed."

–KJV

Faith truly is meant to be blind.

19

IF YOU KNEW HE WAS REALLY COMING

I just started thinking about an event which I would love to be a spectator to some day. It was a question, one that could reshape the world in an instant if only it were taken seriously. The question is this: What would we do differently if we knew Jesus was really coming back?

This should be a no-brainer for anyone who believes that Jesus is no joke. In fact, lots of things should kick into high gear in your life and back flip into a more respectable reality.

So, let's pretend now that you personally know He's coming back and you want to make the best impression. Heck, even I am not bold enough to say that I have no room for improvement. So, let me put it this way: This is what I would do if I knew He was coming back, for real, like anytime soon. Here are my thoughts put into a list that I'd like to call my: "JINJ Reality Check."

Hmm... where to launch from? I think I'll start off on a small scale and let it grow into the monster that it is:

#1. I think that I let small matters bother me that really shouldn't cause me to even raise an eyebrow.

So there it is, the beginning. This is how small issues turn into big ones, and I think we are all responsible for allowing the snowball effect of problems to even exist. You know the scenario: There's the lid off the jar, and it was asked that it be kept tightly sealed. But no, there it is in the middle of the living room for all the world to see! Glancing into the kitchen, another jar is calling out to be noticed. My mouth opens, and before my brain can control its actions, a quick huff escapes my lungs, showing my disgust. Whether I decide to actually voice my disgust or keep my eyebrows folded until a headache grabs hold, I'm still displeased.

What a silly thing to get upset about, having some jars left open that I made a point to tell others to keep closed. Countries are at war, children are dying, someone's cat got run over, and here I am upset about an open jar!

I used to let myself get bent out of shape for teeny-weeny little offenses like that, but not exactly concerning jars, of course, not with my personal messy habits.

I can just imagine Jesus walking in the door as I'm raising an open jar in the air, ruining someone else's day because of my little inconvenience! What a Judgment Day that would be for me to have to explain my unforgiving nature at that moment, not to mention being embarrassed about the whole incident.

All I can say is that I'm glad every time I'm untidy — I don't have to hear about it from God or know I gave Him a headache from His raised eyebrows. But still, I know I have to keep an eye out on not letting little things bother me to any extent.

Okay, still looking down my list of things to do (and not to do):

#2. Don't get involved in the hurting game.

I don't care if I'm driving down the street and someone cuts me off, but sometimes I'd like to return the favor and ruin their mood or cause them to do panic braking for a moment! When someone appears to hurt my feelings or change my mood, it feels personal. I think to myself, *I really look at other people's perspective and try to avoid being a pain to another, as much as possible. So why would someone come out of nowhere and make a rude push my way?*

This isn't fully the eye-for-an-eye mentality (okay, maybe it is). It's more like someone hurts my feelings by their actions with seemingly no remorse; I have little to talk to them about. If someone tries to push me from behind to go faster on the freeway, maybe I should slow down. If someone who I date forgets that I hate coconut and brings that in a shake, I might forget ketchup for their fries next time for them.

Petty, petty, petty stuff, isn't it?

I wouldn't literally do all that I listed. Hmm, well not the last one about the ketchup, because that would just be plain mean. For me, it's just a way of thinking on how to protect myself against bullies and numbskulls.

The question is, are these really purposeful acts of bullying? I've observed that most people are just space cadets, unaware of the damage they cause to another's feelings as they go about their day. It's not really personal; it's just another person trying to get by you in life while doing their own thing with their existence and in the space that they occupy. Most people aren't trying to aim for my head to take me out with a psychological insult!

Yipes! I sound like a paranoid weirdo for even thinking of such a thing. Then again, is it really so rare that I (or anyone else) feels that way at some point in time, when something small or large was done that brought a person's mood down?

People are essentially decent, but don't get me wrong, there *are* some oddballs out there with lesser consciousness about your feelings.

Jesus would be shocked and horrified to know that I took offense to so much by so many people who are under His care, too. I would imagine He would know them better than I would and could school me on how each person was poorly judged on my part, no matter how I interpreted a situation. I'm certain that even

157

those who repeatedly offend others have a great lump of qualities which I am simply unaware of. In judging that offensive person then, I am sure that I would only be hurting myself if I had any thoughts of retaliation.

That just reminded me of something. You know, I got to know this certain group of people who are often judged freely for their outward appearance. *"Not in America,"* you're thinking, right? Darn, Skippy, *especially* in America! You know, the country of no single identity where we keep track of each group, perhaps, to make sure that none gets too big.

Believe it or not, the group I'm talking about goes outside of race and toward a way of living and expression. These are the people who like to tattoo and pierce themselves until they run out of spaces on their bodies. For some of these decorative folks, even hygiene is not always a big factor for the traveling street-kid type. When looking at them from a distance, people might think they are all substance abusers with absolutely no goals in life.

Tauntings, stares, threats, and laughter are often pointed in their direction by those who most often are a part of the younger generation. If you had an occasion to approach one of these people, you might be surprised by who is hiding under all of the body decorations.

I was fortunate enough to talk with a few of them and have found many of them want to look different just to show they are different from society as a whole. They are free and loving individuals who would rather stand out instead of camouflaging themselves in order to blend in with society, as if that would mean they agree with how things are run these days.

Imagine that, allowing your thoughts and attitude to show through literally onto your skin! I thought that was a neat concept. But if we don't have the definition of what's being displayed by getting to know the person, we still would be at a loss. So, until we all know what lies beneath the skin of a person with their intentions intact, no one's motives or soul can be judged simply by looking at the exterior.

So, I've learned to try and find out the reasoning behind what I'm feeling coming my way, although I haven't mastered it yet. But I wouldn't want Jesus to see I wasn't trying to make an effort to be an understanding person. It's so much easier being this way, too. It takes less out of me to show that someone's actions might have hurt me. Big smiles are so much simpler to dish out.

Next on my list:

#3. Being more involved with the problems I see.

It's so easy for me to think that someone else is helping to clean up our city's neighborhoods, so I won't have to worry about it. I could easily see the tumbleweeds of garbage blowing down the streets all the time, but I never thought to hop out of my car and race to pick them up. This is more of a literal topic which I am sure we all have seen but might not have even given a second thought.

Speaking of being literal, I once worked with some folks who were shocked that another person they knew actually drove through a main street that they considered to be a bad neighborhood. I am talking about a 6:00 A.M. drive through a neighborhood that I knew and drove through all the time. It wasn't the best neighborhood, but it sure wasn't worth the drive to go around this whole middle section of the city to get to work, just to avoid the area. It sounded a bit extreme to hear that this was what everyone else did to get to work every day. It was just beyond my comprehension, personally.

Then a little saying I've heard many times before crossed my mind, "Out of sight, out of mind." If you don't see something, you aren't aware of it, and, therefore, it doesn't exist. It was as if some kind of problem was solved, because these co-workers of mine were able to drive around the mentally troubling neighborhoods.

With the tumbleweeds of trash blowing down the streets, everyone could see this happening, but they did nothing. It is almost as if a mental block is assembled in our minds where we see it, but don't process that something should be done about it. Had we trained ourselves to not see it anymore, practically programming ourselves that it's the norm to exist?

While hearing the chatter among my co-workers about the long distance mental and literal roadblock they had conjured up for themselves, I went into "wish mode". I imagined how great it would be if everyone did their part, where we could all stamp out there even being a "needy people" who lived in these more desperate areas. Where there are poor, there are needs that are not being met.

If you had a need for years of your life, you might look at your neighbor or someone driving by who has what you need. Not everyone in this situation thinks that way, of course, but apparently some do. Call it being a thief, filling a need or want, or providing for your family, you just might be inclined to take something from someone who has more than you do.

Poor people and poor areas exist because they have been allowed to exist. Someone has to work for someone else in order for one of us to be on top. Why do you think we can say "inner city" in America and all know it's the place for less fortunate people? The inner city is where the older, run-down, and unwanted homes and buildings are, so of course we allow the poor to live there.

There's a distinct transition in the city of Milwaukee where I live between a poorer neighborhood and a "well-to-do" area. You can literally drive from one block to the next and see rusty cars and run-down homes on one block, and then fancy houses and cars on the next. If Jesus were to come to Milwaukee and travel down this street, I wonder how He might approach the neighbors in that area.

A quick, firm knock at the door of the poor man's house would have to be done, since the doorbell is out of order and a screen door doesn't exist. A cautious man might peek out of the window first and ask who it is before daring to open the door.

At the richer man's home, Jesus would have to be patient as He would ring a doorbell that might chime the song of "It's a Small World (after all)". After waiting several minutes for the richer man to finally reach that wing of the house, Jesus' expression might be interesting, peering through an iron rod screened door.

I'm just taking a wild guess here, but I think Jesus might ponder why there wasn't more equality in the manner of living between these neighbors. Would the richer man even have a sense of responsibility for his poorer neighbor? Would the poorer man feel he hadn't done all he could to become more successful?

I would imagine there could be a sense of guilt that comes over those who fare better than their neighbors, if Jesus were to come now.

Even I've thought about what I would do if that would happen to me, with the poorer places being in existence all over the world. I've accepted that I cannot change the world, and my giving up all that I have wouldn't balance out this planet. The one thing that comforts me is knowing that if I make a wholehearted effort to help with the well-being of another, then I am doing my part.

To truly put the effort forward to help someone get ahead emotionally, physically, spiritually, financially, mentally, or whatever else, I'm giving of myself in some form. Looking at the outside and how physically poor someone might live might not be the thing that needs tending to most. Help someone help themselves. Bring a person to their feet and help them stand strong and independent.

I use God's example in this philosophy because He is a God of resource. God could use a mere thought to materialize all that we need, but instead He brings the materials to us that can be used to create what we need in our lives.

When Moses needed the waters to part so that he and his people could cross, God didn't just zap the water to make it disappear. He used resources; even the winds were used as a form of getting what was needed for Moses and his people.

So maybe we might help our neighbors create a scholarship for a particular neighborhood so the children there can get an education. Donate your time to tutoring, paint someone's house, or give some clothes or furniture to someone less fortunate.

People who are afraid to drive through these poorer neighborhoods don't know the struggles or the goodness in these areas because they haven't taken the time to find out.

The friendliest neighbors I ever had were while living in such a neighborhood. I'd just moved from a place I lived for several years and had only one neighbor approach me in all of that time. The first week in this supposedly "poorer" area I met most of my neighbors, and nearly every day I came home I was greeted by the neighborhood kids with hugs and hellos. This was a neighborhood rich with warmth and protectiveness for those who lived there.

Every little effort counts in helping and meeting neighbors. The funny thing is, if you make your effort in Jesus' name, you will have nothing to fear. I've found that many people like to keep Jesus close at heart, so it seems that He's already built a bridge for us to meet halfway in understanding. Getting involved sounds easier than it is for most, but once it's started, the positive vibes it produces can be addictive.

Personally, I have been giving of myself, but I always think there has to be more that I can do. I've started with one angle and have been continuing with it as best as I can. My angle of spiritual help is my goal, and I hope to spread that out into more angles as I'm able.

As I said, giving is addictive and new ideas to help are addictive as well. Honestly, I can hardly wait to see where it all goes!

I know that there's so much I can do better in knowing that Jesus truly is coming. I know I can never be a perfect individual and I know I am not expected to be. If I were expected to be, then I would have the perfect skin and smile with the perfect attitude and the perfect response to everything. Instead, I'm full of flaws in a lot of the things I do much of the time. It's a good thing I know where my main focus is, and that's my heart, and my heart is devoted to God, Jesus' goals, and to becoming a decent human being.

All along in this chapter I've been saying, "If Jesus were coming, I would do this differently." Well, I am not saying that in a hypothetical sense anymore. The fact of the matter is: He is coming! To some people, including myself, He has always been here and continually makes His presence known.

So my best advice is to "act like you know!" You've heard the stories, heard the preaching, and see the signs all around you that something is about to go down. Who knows when and how all of this will take place? The important thing to know is that it will.

So, in the tradition of the bumper stickers I've seen around that say, "Jesus Is Coming, Look Busy," try realizing that you won't fool Him with surface changes. Instead, get busy making some soul-altering changes.

20

THE FINAL CHAPTER: TAH-DAH!

Joel:
2:28 "And it shall come to pass afterward, that I will pour out my spirit upon all flesh; and your sons and your daughters shall prophesy, your old men shall dream dreams, your young men shall see visions:"

2:29 "And also upon the servants and upon the handmaids in those days will I pour out my spirit."

2:30 "And I will shew wonders in the heavens and in the earth, blood, and fire, and pillars of smoke."

2:31 "The sun shall be turned into darkness, and the moon into blood, before the great and the terrible day of the Lord come."

2:32 "And it shall come to pass, that whosoever shall call on the name of the Lord shall be delivered: for in mount Zion and in Jerusalem shall be deliverance, as the Lord hath said, and in the remnant whom the Lord shall call."

—KJV

According to the Bible, the Spirit of The Lord would come to people in dreams and visions just before the "Day of The Lord." Perhaps this means that this is the time when Jesus would return, which is perceived in the New Testament as the end times. Yet, so many people say that the times we live in are the times of false prophets trying only to make a buck. So, are these critics sure of their stance on all such people with dreams or visions? Besides, who are these so-called critics, and why do we have to even hear about them as if we need them to help form our own opinions? I could never understand that. A "critic" who might be the unkempt but educated loner down the street who writes a superb article of criticism on visions, then people go ahead and quote this man and his single critical thoughts like he's a prophet himself.

I understand how questions can be raised about a person's motives, with so many people out there who are not being true to their word while making prophecies about events to come in this world. No doubt some of these people are distractions who only draw spectators to have faith in someone else besides God, and the critics do no less.

Instead of avoiding these types of issues, I think it's best to be real about them and talk about it like it is. I know where my heart is, and I know that I have been true to my word on what I have been shown and told by Jesus. I've gone through the whole "why me" bit and wondering how I will be viewed by others for speaking about seeing such a tremendous soul. I just think it's important for people to truly know the reality and impact of what I am trying to relate here.

There are some questions that each of us have to bring up so that we can all make a wise decision on whether to accept what's in front of us or not. Rest assured, there are more people out there than just me who are chatting about having seen Jesus. There are increasing reports of holy visions going on in the world in many different forms and situations.

Another phenomenon that people in general are not aware of are the strange dreams which many people are having about cataclysmic events. Yeah, that's right; it doesn't end with just holy visions. The verse above from the Book of Joel doesn't specify what the dreams, prophecies, or visions will all be about, but it did say:

2:30 "And I will shew wonders in the heavens and in the earth, blood, and fire, and pillars of smoke."

Many people, including myself, are having tremendous dreams of great floods, wars, destroyed cities, meteors striking the Earth, earthquakes, and other dooming tragedies. These dreams are much like the waking dreams where they are so real that they are hard to keep out of one's mind.

Do they just happen to be common worries of people that the world will end soon, or are we being prepared for something?

When soldiers begin in the military, they are put in pretend situations and simulation drills on what to do when the enemy is approaching. By going through drills like this, the soldiers are less likely to panic if they are ever put into the actual situation so they are able to respond appropriately.

In the cataclysmic dreams people are having, they feel directed on what to do or are given scenario hints on what can happen. The question is, are these dreams being given as a warning so we are more prepared and will react in a more calm and rational manner?

After having some of these dreams, I feel they get categorized in my memory as events of experience. They feel so close to being real that if I were to be put in that same dreamed situation, I know that I would react in a more educated manner on what to do. What an impact a supposed "meaningless" dream can have!

Just as the quote I have in the beginning of this book states: "The prophet that hath a dream, let him tell a dream; and he that hath my word, let him speak my word faithfully." (*Jeremiah* 23:28 –KJV)

I interpret this phrase as directly pointing to the distinction between a dream and God's Word. If you had a cool dream, feel free to share it if you want, as long as it is not meant to distract from God, His Word, or His Purpose. But if you have God's Word, talk about it with faith in knowing that it came from Him. Yet, nothing and no one's words or reports are to replace what has already been written of concerning God or Jesus. I have only offered an additional affirmation of encouragement for people whom I share this existence with to truly realize the Reality of Jesus. I firmly believe that what I've related here is true to the best of my knowledge, heart, and faith.

Being a person of faith is a dedication of one's self. Sure, you have the choice to share your insight or not, but if it came from God, there is a good chance that it can help another person. In that sense, if God chatted with you about something or if Jesus dropped by, responsibility once again comes into play — hugely!

I hope I owned up to the challenge and shared the messages that came my way in the best possible format. I have always embraced humor as being a comfort giver for most situations or topics. Some might think that it's not always appropriate, but even Jesus has a sense of humor. So, if some folks take my manner in sharing my story as being out of place, well then, I think more joy needs to come their way, since nothing was done with poor intentions.

In the past, had I read a book of this nature, I would have thought that the author was continually throwing her hands up in praise, something like I've seen on television or in church. But here I sit, with my hands down to my sides still, and my heart is just as dedicated without moving around too much. If I reach over my shoulder to scratch my back where my shirt tag is currently scratching me, even then, I can still be just as strong for Jesus.

I want to get across that it matters what you do on the inside in directing your heart, even if you are going through the good motions of helping someone. Helping someone out can't be done as a job, where you hope to get a fat paycheck at the end of your life. It needs to be a part of you that pays you in good feelings as you go along.

That's the big payoff.

I am forever grateful that I got the chance to see Jesus, even had I only caught a glimpse of Him. Seeing Him four times brings my gratitude beyond levels of comprehension. I could make one of my rambling lists of Jesus' generous intentions here, but I think I have bombarded you enough with them.

Wow, I can't believe that I'm coming around the corner, reaching the stretch in finishing this book. My mind searches and searches for some colossal point that I can leave you with before this all ends.

Believe it or not, I actually just have one to mention here, and it's a little bit preachy — like you didn't see that one coming:

All of this "Jesus is coming" talk comes down to a choice. We all have a choice if we want to follow the teachings of Jesus — or not. We can believe He is coming soon or some time way in the future. We can also decide if our particular faith even allows the thought that Jesus was anyone special.

There are tons of faiths out there with even more tons of rules that people believe God has to act according to, or else we won't accept His miracles. I found this especially to be the case with my having these visits from Jesus. I often get questioned by people if I tested Him or if He did something in a certain manner, since only then would I know it was actually Jesus visiting me.

Isn't that something? Who knew there was a science of getting to know what is God related, even when it states in the Bible that all men's hearts (from the least to the greatest, Hebrews 8:11) will know The Lord? I think it just goes to show how this society wants to use more head than heart, and more flesh than soul, in our approaches to accepting God.

I don't always understand who makes these rules when God is the Number One Rule Maker and has a creativity which none of us can even imagine. So, if placing God or Jesus within a line of rules is the best a person can do to ignore all of the witness testimonies today and in the past, we should all focus our prayers for that person.

Tolerance of other people's beliefs is important, even while following our own personal choices, since we can't make the choice for others. Sharing what we feel to be the truth about God, with just the right touch, shouldn't be harmful, though. Sharing should always be done with respect and with no forcing, cramming, pushing, or shoving.

We all have the right to choose to follow a faith or not, but I know this much: In America, being ignorant of a law doesn't render you innocent if you violate that law. Meaning, if you broke that law, you'll be charged with those offenses without mercy.

Yipes! Not knowing about God's Son, I really couldn't even imagine how offensive that is. So, at least being informed about Jesus is a start for a person who's not into Him just yet.

I just couldn't imagine facing Him without knowing the first thing about Him, but I also know that it wasn't hard to recognize Him for who He was and is.

Still, I suggest people get to know the man, the Son, the Savior, the jolly friend named Jesus! Knowing Him is the best thing that ever happened to me.

I was going to throw a wisecrack in here, but for once I actually thought it would be inappropriate. Wow, He really has changed who I am, for me to refrain from doing that! ☺

See, you are witnessing history in the making as you read along here, so there's some Jesus proof for you already!

I don't even know how to end this, to be honest with you, because the topic of Jesus is something pretty darned endless. What should I say, "Get ready; He's coming, and I can hardly wait for that to happen?" No, you already can see in my writings that I'm looking forward to that day.

So, I think I should probably end off much the same way I began this book which is so full of my thoughts, humor, and love for Him.

Jesus!

What a name, and one that is surely no joke!

Unfathomable blessings and best of love to you all — in Jesus' name — of course!

~ Heidi Hollis~

ABOUT THE AUTHOR

For over 20 years, Heidi Hollis has been involved in looking into mysterious topics from a very young age. She is an advocate for bringing extraordinary topics to a comfortable level where they can be spoken of frankly and openly without shame— even with a hint of humor! She has written for various publications and is sought worldwide for her levelheaded advice and research into many of the world's intriguing phenomena.

She has also appeared on numerous national and international radio and television programs and often hosts radio talk shows, such as Heidi Hollis-The Outlander, on Spirit Guide Radio powered by CBS Radio's The Sky and Heidi HOLLERS! (with Heidi Hollis). Her previous book, *The Secret War,* is the first book ever written on the newer phenomenon of Shadow People and the ties that aliens have to angels and demons; Hollis instructs readers how to protect themselves against various types of negative encounters and how Jesus can be called upon for guaranteed help. Her book, *Picture Prayers*, expands upon her revelation shared in JINJ, where she details how we can all learn how to pray like the angels (as she was taught by an angel) and communicate with God and others on a more natural level beyond all assumed limitations.

In addition, Hollis is a practicing occupational therapist, columnist, lecturer, and an accomplished comic strip and 3D ceramic artist.

Visit her sites
www.HeidiHollis.com
www.JesusIsNoJoke.com
www.PicturePrayers.com

www.ingramcontent.com/pod-product-compliance
Lightning Source LLC
Chambersburg PA
CBHW070414090426
42733CB00009B/1667